Careers for You Series

CAREERS FOR

GOOD SAMARITANS

& Other Humanitarian Types

MARJORIE EBERTS
MARGARET GISLER

THIRD EDITION

McGraw-Hill

New York   Chicago   San Francisco   Lisbon   London   Madrid   Mexico City
Milan   New Delhi   San Juan   Seoul   Singapore   Sydney   Toronto

The **McGraw·Hill** Companies

Library of Congress Cataloging-in-Publication Data

Eberts, Marjorie.
    Careers for good samaritans & other humanitarian types / Marjorie Eberts,
  Margaret Gisler.— 3rd ed.
      p. cm. — (McGraw-Hill careers for you series)
    ISBN 0-07-145879-4 (alk. paper)
    1. Human services—Vocational guidance—United States.   2. Social
  service—Vocational guidance—United States.   I. Gisler, Margaret.   II. Title.

   HV10.5.E24 2006
   361.0023'73—dc22
                                               2005025278

· ·

To Edda Fisher, Dr. James Travers, Father
Martin Brennan, S.J., and all the other
Good Samaritans and humanitarians
who have made the world a better place
through their unselfish actions

1 2 3 4 5 6 7 8 9 0 DOC/DOC 0 9 8 7 6

ISBN 0-07-145879-4

McGraw-Hill books are available at special quantity discounts to use as premiums and
sales promotions, or for use in corporate training programs. For more information,
please write to the Director of Special Sales, Professional Publishing, McGraw-Hill,
Two Penn Plaza, New York, NY 10121-2298. Or contact your local bookstore.

This book is printed on acid-free paper.

Contents

Foreword

....

As a young man coming of age in the seventies in Gary, Indiana, during the height of the War on Poverty, I saw the powerful role that government had in driving our nation's spirit of service and civic engagement. Initiatives determined to make a difference in the lives of the less fortunate ranged from Head Start for preschool children to Foster Grandparents for older Americans to economic development initiatives focused on inner cities and economically distressed rural areas. They all proliferated during this era. When I was young, my late father introduced me to the nature of public service during his tenure as an employee of the city of Gary, a role which brought him great pride and joy.

Equally, I learned the nature of compassion and importance of service to others through my faith, from the passage in Luke 12:48, "For everyone to whom much is given, of him shall much be required," to the Christian definition of charity as "The pure love of Christ; love, compassion, service, sympathy and concern for others." The powerful notion of caring and service to others has played an important role in both my vocation and personal life.

During my academic career as a student at Indiana University, I learned of the origins of service and civic engagement as a function of citizenship. My initial work experience at a statewide nonprofit social services organization while still in college provided me a foundation of practical experience for a career in public service. There I learned the important concept of individual responsibility and the pragmatic or "how to" of helping others through the structure of state and federally funded programs. Now, some three decades later, those lessons still resonate and inform my daily work as an administrator with the Corporation for National and Community Service. Those lessons make it possible to exercise my commitment to humanity while responsibly carrying out the public trust.

As a college professor at Indiana University School of Public and Environmental Affairs, I teach a capstone course, a concluding class for graduating seniors preparing for their careers in public service. As important as the skills necessary to navigate the public and nonprofit sectors is the reason behind selecting public service as a vocation. I challenge students to identify their motivation—what is their driving force for seeking a career in the field? More than often the answer is to obtain a better job and to enjoy a good quality of life. For a few though, there is a passion beyond a job and career—a devotion to making a difference in the lives of others and in their communities. These individuals receive satisfaction from improving the human condition and possess an overriding concern for humanity. It is my belief that this embodies the true spirit of public service and manifests the expectations of citizenship by our founders. The knowledge that, as citizens, when we help our neighbors, we help ourselves. So to those model citizens and "good deed doers" everywhere, I thank you and encourage you to continue on this path with hopes that three decades later you, too, will find it as fulfilling as I have.

Louis Lopez, M.P.A.
State Director for Indiana
Corporation for National and Community Service

CHAPTER ONE

Life Paths for Good Samaritans and Humanitarians

"Choose a job you love, and you will never have to work a day in your life."
—Confucius

The list of Good Samaritans and other humanitarian types who have built careers around their concern for others is endless. Furthermore, close to one hundred million people in the United States are volunteering their time each year serving in soup kitchens, acting as mentors to disadvantaged youths, visiting nursing homes, building houses for the homeless, and otherwise answering the call to better the lives of others. The options for people who want to make a career helping others are limitless. There is a constant need for people to do fund-raising, accounting, or public relations for organizations that help make life better for others.

Good Samaritans and humanitarians recognize that the challenges we face today are great both in the United States and around the world. Millions of people live in poverty and lack the basic necessities of life. Hunger is not just a reality for people living in third world countries—it exists at a frightening level in this country. Millions of people are overwhelmed with such social problems as homelessness, drug addiction, teenage pregnancy, domestic violence, single parenting, crime, illiteracy, gangs, and unemployment. More than thirteen million people in the world are refugees, exiled from their homes or homeland by war, earthquakes, monsoons, drought, and famine. The ecological plight of our planet is described every day in newspaper headlines about the pollution of our air and water, deforestation, and the consequences of global warming. And despite two world wars in the past hundred years, peace remains an elusive goal as conflict continues in too many places in the world.

While the list of problems seems overwhelming, successes have been tallied because Good Samaritans and other humanitarians have chosen careers that are leading to solutions. Through their work, they have responded to human needs and improved the welfare and happiness of others. Training coordinators at Goodwill Industries have helped the disabled and disadvantaged obtain jobs so they can become independent and self-sufficient. Leaders of YWCA programs have shown elderly women how to explore and use their skills and abilities. Hygiene educators with CARE have taught villagers in third world countries how to maintain their health. Red Cross workers have given classes that help parents learn the skills essential to successfully rearing their children. The professional staff of Volunteers of America is running nonprofit housing complexes, halfway houses for alcohol and drug abusers, and shelters for adolescent runaways. Social workers are helping the elderly, mentally ill, abused, and others who are seriously in need. UNICEF staffers are tackling the causes of death and disease among children under five. Doctors and nurses are working in federally funded health-care clinics for the homeless. Chaplains are counseling the incarcerated.

Making Your Mark in the World

As a Good Samaritan or humanitarian type, you have the opportunity to choose from a large number of careers that will help solve the world's problems. You can have a career that has social value. Good Samaritans and humanitarians can help people find jobs, work on crisis hotlines, teach at-risk students, minister to the spiritual needs of others, counsel women in abuse situations, aid disaster victims, raise funds to fight diseases, and orient refugees to new countries. There are also positions for people who want to be involved in social movements—especially political and environmental groups. You can advance a variety of causes, from human rights to saving endangered species to arms control. The choice is yours. You can make a difference to individuals, families, community groups, and society as a whole by working in a career that will create a better world.

Although you can find a job almost anywhere in the world that will appeal to your altruistic impulse, the greatest variety of jobs is found in large urban areas. Your choice extends to working in social service organizations ranging from the giant American Red Cross to a small agency; being employed by a federal, state, or local government unit or even an international organization; or serving as a caring medical, legal, or religious professional.

If your aim in life is to get rich, working as a Good Samaritan or humanitarian is not the right choice for you. You simply will not make the huge salaries of Wall Street wonders, Hollywood luminaries, sports stars, and high-profile doctors and lawyers. Nevertheless, your economic outlook is not bleak.

If you work for the government, you can usually count on long-term job security and good benefits, especially vacation and sick-leave benefits. In addition, salaries at large nonprofit organizations are rapidly becoming competitive with those in the government and the private sector. Top managers at large nonprofit organizations may earn more than $100,000 a year. This, of course, is far more than most people employed in these organizations earn. The lowest salaries are paid by the small nonprofit organizations that have jobs with the least security and by such government programs as AmeriCorps and the Peace Corps. As you might guess, professionals such as doctors, lawyers, nurses, and accountants can generally expect to earn less working for the government or for nonprofit organizations than if they are employed in the private sector. Most Good Samaritans and humanitarians, however, find that they are decided winners in the category of job satisfaction.

An Overview of Occupations for Good Samaritans

Good Samaritans and other humanitarians can find careers that offer real satisfaction. Many jobs allow them to use their skills to make the world a better place for others. Mother Teresa, Eleanor Roosevelt, Florence Nightingale, Jane Addams, Albert Schweitzer, and Nelson Mandela are just a few of the well-known Good Samaritans and humanitarians who have made unique contributions to the world through their work. You can join them. As Dr. Martin Luther King Jr. said, "Everybody can be great because anybody can serve."

This book is designed to help all altruistic people find careers in which they can take their consciences to work. Here is an overview of some of the careers that you will read about in this book.

Career Opportunities in Social Service Organizations

Where you go to work makes a difference. A job at Microsoft or General Motors may not give you the same satisfaction as one at the American Red Cross, Goodwill Industries, Junior Achievement, CARE, or Volunteers of America. Within these large social service organizations, every job contributes in some way to the worthwhile work of the organization. In addition to these well-known social service organizations, there are thousands of smaller organizations with much narrower missions. For example, the Harriet Tubman Center in Minneapolis, Minnesota, leads battered women and their children to freedom from abusive situations. No matter how you wish to help others, some organization is probably devoted to the same mission.

Careers with the Government

The problems that poverty brings are enormous: homelessness, hunger, poor health, illiteracy, crime, and abuse. The United States launched what is popularly called "The War on Poverty" in the 1960s and greatly increased the number of government programs to help the poor. While many of these programs have been cut back and some have been eliminated, government units remain a very large source of jobs for Good Samaritans and humanitarians. At all levels of the government, jobs that will let you help others are found in an incredible number of areas, as few social needs are not addressed by some government program.

Jobs with the government are not limited to locations in the United States. Today, approximately sixty-five hundred Peace Corps volunteers are working in almost ninety countries. Americans are also working abroad for other agencies that have economic, health, and development programs to assist the needy around the world. Besides jobs abroad with the United States government, international organizations such as the United Nations have jobs for Good Samaritans throughout the world.

Careers in the Medical Field

Mother Teresa is a symbol of the good that medical Good Samaritans and humanitarians can do. While doctors, nurses, and other medical workers focus on helping the sick, there are some medical jobs that truly require the special compassion and devotion of Good Samaritans. These jobs are found in caring for the poor and homeless in inner-city clinics, the dying in hospices, the victims of AIDS, and the unfortunate in third world countries. These are challenging jobs that are not typically found in the antiseptic quarters of modern hospitals. And they typically involve dispensing loving care as well as medical care.

Careers with Religious Groups

A strong desire to serve God and to help others draws people into religious careers. While a career with a religious group often focuses on preaching and teaching, such a career may also involve working in the social welfare network of a religious organization, which includes jobs in prisons, soup kitchens, shelters for the homeless, hospitals, and centers for alcoholics and drug addicts. For some, a career with a religious group may mean traveling abroad as a missionary to spread the doctrine of faith and improve the living condition of others. There are also those who choose to live in religious communities.

Serving as a Volunteer

The Points of Light Foundation was founded in May 1990 during the presidency of George H. W. Bush to engage more people effectively in volunteer community service to help solve serious social problems. In April 1997, all the living presidents or their representatives joined together at a summit to ask every caring citizen to volunteer time to help children in need. The focus of American presidents on volunteerism as a way to improve the quality of life underlines the importance of this special commitment. Today, millions of people are excited about using their skills, talents, spare time, and energy to work as volunteers to do some good.

Working as a volunteer is an excellent way for Good Samaritans and humanitarians to investigate different careers. It is also an opportunity to gain experience that could lead to a job. A limitless variety of jobs is available to volunteers. Teaching young children to read, working in a soup kitchen, leading a scout troop, helping at a nursing home, answering crisis-line calls, or helping save endangered species are just a few of the options.

More Careers for Good Samaritans and Humanitarians

Throughout the United States, Good Samaritans and humanitarians are increasingly finding careers that center on making the world a better place. Many have elected to work at foundations, overseeing the awarding of grants or running a program. Some have chosen to work as teachers, doctors, and lawyers, ministering to those most in need of their services. A few have found careers as entrepreneurs, filling a wide variety of needs—from building low-income housing to providing fuel to the poor. The list of jobs for Good Samaritans and humanitarians is a list of intriguing possibilities.

Job Qualifications

Organizations are not going to hire you solely because you are a compassionate person who wants to do good. A concern for others is certainly a prerequisite for someone who wants to work for an organization dedicated to humanitarian work, but more is required. You need to demonstrate that you can work effectively with people who have serious problems. You especially need to have a sense of humor to be able to put into perspective some of the difficult situations you are likely to encounter on the job. And for most jobs, you need to demonstrate good communication skills. Besides an ability to talk easily with people, you may also need good writing skills so you can create program and funding proposals and produce accurate, easy-to-read reports. Humanitarian organizations usually generate a great deal of paperwork, requiring the possession of solid clerical skills. Because we now live in a computer-oriented world, you should be familiar with using a personal computer, at least for basic word processing. For many jobs, you also need to be able to handle spreadsheets and databases as well as send e-mail.

Competition for jobs at humanitarian organizations is often quite intense. You need to have solid personal and professional skills. Many organizations prefer to hire people with work experience, which may be your biggest hurdle to getting your first job. Fortunately, most organizations consider volunteer or intern experience a satisfactory substitute for paid work experience. Job seekers can get head starts on their careers by volunteering or serving as interns while they are in high school or college.

You can find a job in humanitarian organizations with only a high school diploma, but the path to getting a job and advancing to top positions is much smoother for college graduates. And for many positions, including the very highest positions, a master's degree is rapidly becoming a necessity.

Finding a Job

Studying newspaper ads, contacting college placement offices, sending resumes to organizations, and talking to people you know are all time-tested ways to find jobs. Organizations often utilize the Internet to advertise open positions, either on the agency's website or other career-based websites. There are also some special information sources that people seeking jobs in humanitarian organizations should use.

- Visit the United Way office in your community and ask to see a community services directory. This directory lists the local nonprofit and government agencies and describes their services. The directory will give you valuable names, addresses, and phone numbers of individuals and organizations to contact in your job search. If your local United Way branch does not publish such a directory, the staff will be able to tell you who does publish this information in your community.
- Use the Internet in your job search. You will find that the larger organizations have Web pages describing their mission, recent activities, and—most importantly—employment information. In some cases, you can even apply for jobs online. Furthermore, finding out about a job on the Net lets employers know you have Internet know-how. There are even spots on the Net where you can post your resume at no charge.

- A very high percentage of available jobs in the nonprofit sector are never advertised. They are filled by people who are friends or acquaintances of people who are already working for the organization or are known by the organization. Through volunteering and internships, you can begin to meet people who may be in a position to help you find a job.
- Certain periodicals on nonprofit and humanitarian works have listings of jobs and internships in addition to news and feature articles on the latest developments, conferences, and grants. You can get a better picture of your employment marketplace by looking at the *NonProfit Times*, *The Chronicle of Philanthropy*, and *Foundation News*.

Making the World a Better Place

You can make your voice heard. You can do something to help the people who live on Earth. No matter whether you are concerned about the homeless, illiterate, drug addicts, working poor, hungry, refugees, pollution, or endangered species, you can find a job that will make a difference.

"You must be the change you wish to see in the world."
—Gandhi

CHAPTER TWO

Strengthening and Building Communities Through Nonprofit Organizations

ood Samaritans and other humanitarian types know that where you go to work makes a difference. For many, careers in social service organizations may be their dream. No matter whether their skills are used in directly helping others or simply managing or doing the everyday work of the organization, they are making a contribution to the individuals the program serves. In this way, the employees of social service organizations are able to help the homeless, the abused, the substance addicted, the elderly, low-income families, the disabled, and the illiterate. They join the roster of people throughout history who have endeavored to help and share with those in need.

The History of Social Service Organizations

Historically, people simply volunteered their services one-to-one. The first organizations devoted to helping people were the major religious organizations that began providing care for the sick and feeding the poor during the Middle Ages. After the Industrial Revolution reached the United States in the 1800s, this country started changing from a nation of people living in small towns and on farms to a nation of people living in cities and working in industry. Soon the cities became crowded with workers who were earning very low wages. The problems people encountered in their daily lives became more complicated. In this environment, the first social service agencies designed to help people on an organized basis emerged. It wasn't until after the Civil War, however, that the number of social service organizations increased dramatically. Suddenly, there were groups providing care for the sick, the poor, and immigrants. One of the well-known charitable organizations was Hull House, a settlement house that opened in 1889 and still has active centers in Chicago. Many other familiar organizations, including the Young Women's Christian Association (YWCA), Volunteers of America, Goodwill Industries of America, and the American Red Cross, were also started in the United States in the late 1800s.

Franklin Roosevelt's New Deal in the 1930s and Lyndon Johnson's Great Society in the 1960s greatly increased the role of government in the welfare of all citizens. Surprisingly, these programs did not replace private social service organizations. Instead, they stimulated the growth of such groups, as the government channeled money to them to deliver federally mandated services. New organizations emerged, and older organizations expanded their services. This expansion accelerated in the 1990s as government at all levels reduced its role in welfare.

Organizations providing social services can be designated nonprofit under Section 501(c)(3) of the Internal Revenue Service Code, which means that their services benefit people outside the organization and are supported by contributions from individuals, corporations, foundations, and the government. These organizations also commit any surplus funds to the support of the group's services.

Working in Social Service Organizations

Being part of a social service organization can be very different from working for a business or the government. Social service organizations, unlike businesses, don't rely on making a profit. Nevertheless, money does play a role in the operation of a social service organization. Unlike a government agency, which is federally funded, funds to keep a social service organization running must usually be obtained from a variety of sources. This can be a formidable task; competition for money is keen because the number of social service organizations is very large and is growing even larger.

Perhaps the greatest difference between social service organizations and business and government organizations is in the managerial structure. In most businesses and government agencies, employees are simply told what to do by their bosses. Often, they do not feel as if they have much individual responsibility or ability to bring about changes. At a social service organization, especially a small one, there is likely to be more sharing of authority. Employees frequently have greater responsibility for deciding how their jobs are to be done. Finally, an esprit de corps, a sense of common interests and responsibilities that comes from working with others for a noble cause, is a common characteristic of smaller organizations.

The outlook for jobs is decidedly good in social service organizations. In the nonprofit sector of the economy, the greatest growth in the number of jobs has been in social service organizations. While more jobs are located in the Northeast, jobs exist throughout the country. Within each state, the largest concentration of jobs is in the biggest cities, because this is where the population most needing social services resides.

Overall, more than one million people work in social service organizations. Individual organizations vary enormously in their number of employees. Very large organizations, like the American

Red Cross and the YWCA, employ thousands of people. On the other hand, in a great number of organizations, a single paid employee directs a staff of volunteers. In many social service organizations, volunteers greatly outnumber paid employees.

The variety of social services performed by an organization is closely related to its size; larger organizations tend to offer more social services than smaller ones. Many small organizations concentrate solely on providing one service. The range of services is continually expanding. Following is a partial list of services that are commonly provided by social service agencies:

- adoption services
- child care and education
- clothing and furniture assistance
- consumer protection
- emergency disaster relief
- family counseling and living skills
- financial counseling and loans
- food banks and meals
- housing and shelter
- job counseling and placement
- legal aid
- medical assistance
- pregnancy counseling
- rape counseling
- services for the aging, disadvantaged, handicapped, immigrants, and migrants
- substance-abuse clinics and counseling
- suicide prevention
- support for abused women and children
- transportation service
- youth development

One of the best ways to experience a career in a social service organization is to do volunteer work or to serve as an intern. Not everyone can survive the stress of working with people whose needs are so great. Many people burn out from the overwhelming challenges. As a volunteer or intern, you get a bird's-eye view of what humanitarian work is like, and you can rapidly learn whether your desire for a career as a Good Samaritan or humanitarian is a good personal choice.

Educational Options for Social Service Careers

Not all jobs in social service organizations require degrees from four-year colleges. Some jobs are filled by high school graduates. Many other jobs are filled by individuals holding associate's or two-year degrees from a variety of human service programs and institutions. However, more and more jobs in social service organizations—especially those dealing directly with people—require a bachelor's degree as a condition for employment. It is common for those in social service to hold degrees in social work, psychology, sociology, education, and related fields. An individual who wishes to work specifically as a social worker usually needs a degree in social work as well as licensing by the state.

Because employees with multiple skills are needed in social service organizations, continued schooling beyond the bachelor's degree is commonplace for professionals. In addition, employees in smaller organizations tend to move to larger ones to advance their careers, and such moves may make more classroom training necessary. Sufficient skills cannot always be obtained by on-the-job training. Attending seminars, courses, and workshops is an easy way to upgrade skills and develop new ones. Some of the large national social service organizations—including the American Red Cross, YWCA, YMCA, and Boy Scouts of America—run educational programs for their paid staff as well as volunteers.

One of the largest in-house training programs is operated by the United Way of America's National Academy for Voluntarism

(NAV). Most of the group's programs are run at the National Service and Training Center in Alexandria, Virginia, although programs are also held at other sites around the country. These programs are open to board members, staff, and volunteers of the United Way of America, as well as those from other human service agencies. Each year, about six thousand people, mostly professionals, attend these programs to enhance their career development. The NAV offers courses, workshops, and seminars in such subject areas as communications, community problem solving, finance, fund distribution, general skill development, management, marketing, organization development, resource development, and volunteer development. This schedule of programs extends from the introductory to the executive level. The NAV publishes both a calendar and a catalog with useful information about its programs. You can find out more about NAV programs by writing to:

United Way
National Academy for Voluntarism
701 North Fairfax Street
Alexandria, VA 22314

Another avenue for developing new skills and updating existing skills is through a certificate program. Courses are usually offered at convenient times for working people, and they take place at universities, colleges, and community colleges, frequently as part of a school's continuing education program. You can obtain certificates in areas such as voluntary or nonprofit management, work experience with the handicapped, and fund-raising. At some institutions, course work toward a certificate can be used toward a degree. You can find out about certificate programs by contacting local schools, reading newspaper ads and workplace bulletin boards, and looking at college catalogs in the public library.

Continued professional development through formal course work is almost a necessity. Many career social service employees obtain master's degrees either in a specific area, such as social work, psychology, counseling, or education, or in an area of management. The longer a person works with an organization, the more likely his or her job will become increasingly administrative.

A master's degree in business administration (M.B.A.) is helpful for those people who want to work in such areas as finance, investment, and fund-raising. Considerable specialized expertise is needed by those who are running the largest social service organizations, which may have annual budgets in excess of $500 million. (Of course, the majority of social service organizations have much smaller annual budgets.)

Since the M.B.A. is primarily designed for a career in business, a master's degree in nonprofit administration (M.N.A.) may be a better choice for those wishing to climb higher on the administrative side of the social service career ladder. Unfortunately, there are far more schools offering M.B.A.s than M.N.A.s. Courses in nonprofit management can also be found as part of the curriculum in some graduate schools of public administration.

Behind the Scenes and on the Job in Social Service Organizations

People with good intentions often work in social service organizations. These jobs are perfect for Good Samaritans. Not everyone in these organizations is working directly with the people in need, but the support staff—the secretaries, accountants, lawyers, computer operators, administrators, and even the maintenance workers—feel good about their jobs because their work contributes to fulfilling the altruistic purpose of the organization.

The remainder of this chapter describes both large and small social service organizations, their missions, and some of their programs, as well as the personal work experiences of a number of Good Samaritans and humanitarians. You will find out what these people do in their jobs, how they obtained their jobs, what their future plans are, and how their jobs satisfy their desires to work as Good Samaritans and humanitarians.

First, several larger organizations, with very familiar names, will be discussed. Then a few of the many small social service organizations will be investigated. You will see the wide array of options that exist for Good Samaritans and humanitarians who desire to work in social service organizations.

Young Women's Christian Association

Like several other large social service organizations, the YWCA began in England. In 1855, a group of young women in London joined together to find housing for nurses returning from the Crimean War. Another group was organizing prayer circles at about the same time. The YWCA was officially formed when the two groups united in 1877. A similar organization, known as the Ladies' Christian Association, had been founded in New York City in 1858. In 1866, the first YWCA was organized in Boston, and the organization grew rapidly, especially in large industrial cities.

Today, the YWCA has 8,112 programs in 122 countries, from large cities to rural communities, serving about twenty-five million women worldwide. It has more than two million members and a staff of almost nineteen thousand employees. More than two hundred thousand volunteers serve in many capacities.

A job at the YWCA offers job security plus the opportunity for advancement. The YWCA is a good choice of workplace for Good Samaritans and humanitarians who share the YWCA's twofold mission of empowering women and girls and eliminating racism. Within each community, the YWCA works toward these goals by developing programs reflecting that community's special needs and interests. The YWCA also offers in-house training programs to enhance the careers of both staff and volunteers. In addition to local and regional training programs, the organization has a Leadership Development Center in Phoenix, Arizona, which offers three- to five-day programs.

A YWCA in a Major Metropolitan Area. As the largest nonprofit women's organization in Minneapolis and Saint Paul, the

YWCA employs more than 250 people and has 6,000 members. Ever since it started as a lunchroom and rest area for working women in 1891, the organization has been responsive to community needs. For example, in 1929 the YWCA offered employment services to women who were looking for jobs during the Depression and, during World War II, offered programs for Japanese interned in camps. Today, the Minneapolis YWCA works toward its mission of empowerment and equality in six program areas: the Children's Center, Metro Youth Services, Encore/Women's Health Promotion, Changing Aging, Health and Fitness, and the Ruth Hawkins YWCA Community Center.

The Changing Aging program focuses on older women's issues, concerns, and strengths. Older women are encouraged to explore their skills and abilities, reflect upon their lives from different perspectives, dare to risk new ideas, and continue to contribute to their communities. Until recently, Marla Carlson was the director of the Changing Aging program, in charge of a paid staff of three employees as well as five hundred volunteers. Marla holds a degree in community services, and her assistant, a college graduate, is working on a counseling degree.

Although Marla's job was more administrative than hands-on, she did get to do such things as provide one-on-one counseling and personally escort someone to get a social security card. Her days were always extremely busy as she planned for conferences, arranged education programs, met with advisory groups, testified at hearings on legislation for the aging, and oversaw the publication of a newsletter.

Marla came to Minneapolis with experience in managing a medical clinic in California. Shortly after her arrival in the city, she was volunteering at a community center, helping senior citizens with Medicare forms and insurance forms. One month later, she was offered a job planning programs for the elderly at the center. This job did not offer much contact with people, but Marla's next job with a nutrition program for seniors gave her the opportunity to be a counselor and to train older people to be peer counselors.

When the nutrition program ended seven years later, Marla found a new job as an outreach person and then coordinator at a senior center. Ultimately, she came to the YWCA as director of the Changing Aging program.

Working with the aging throughout most of her career gave Marla an appreciation of their individual stories and their strength to survive adversity. It also offered her the opportunity to help this segment of society by providing much-needed information and support.

One part of Metro Youth Services is Career Pathways, a career development program for eleven- to nineteen-year-olds. Career Pathways concentrates on career awareness, job readiness, decision making, and planning for young people making the transition between school and the workplace. Activities include individual and group counseling, informational interviewing, conferences, retreats, and career clubs.

Candace Samuel served as the coordinator of Career Pathways, implementing every phase of the program. This included working for a class period over the course of six to twelve weeks with small groups of students at local high schools. Candace and the students focused on career exploration and goal setting. Because the students realized that she was sincere in caring for them, Candace was able to make a tangible difference in their lives. Many of the students who participated in her program now have better grades, improved attendance, and a more positive attitude toward school as a result of the program.

Candace believes this job was almost like a calling. She tried to be a positive role model for the inner-city students she counseled. Her interest in helping people developed through her church, and by age thirteen she was working with senior citizens. During high school, she participated in a school program in which she helped elementary schoolchildren with peer pressure, lack of self-esteem, and homework problems. Candace's educational background includes an associate of arts degree in human services, and she is currently working on a bachelor's degree in human services administration. Before obtaining her YWCA job, Candace worked at a community center as a caseworker and as an assistant teacher for at-risk preschoolers.

Goodwill Industries of America

Another social service organization that evolved in the late 1800s was Goodwill Industries of America. Edgar Helms, a Methodist minister, organized the poor and disadvantaged residents of his Boston parish to repair secondhand furniture, clothing, and other items collected from local residents. The goods were then sold at low cost to people with limited incomes, and the proceeds were paid to the workers, who learned job skills and earned money at the same time.

Today, there are autonomous Goodwill Industries in about 207 cities in the United States and Canada and 32 cities overseas in twenty-two countries. More than ninety-three thousand people are employed worldwide. The mission of the organization is now focused on striving to achieve the full participation in society of disabled people and other individuals with special needs. Goodwill Industries aims to help these people by expanding their opportunities and occupational capabilities through a worldwide network of nonprofit, community-based organizations operating in response to local needs.

As the world's largest provider of employment for individuals with barriers to employment, Goodwill Industries offers a great opportunity for those who are specifically interested in providing employment and training services. The current focus is on helping those who are moving from welfare to work. And like any other organization, Goodwill Industries has managerial and administrative positions.

Job Training. Anne Melaas is a training coordinator for Goodwill Industries in a large metropolitan area. She is responsible for coordinating comprehensive job training, placement, and related services for disabled and disadvantaged people, helping them to become independent and self-sufficient. The goal of the job training program is to place trainees in productive jobs in the community as soon as possible.

Anne works with classes of five or six disabled or disadvantaged adults, training them for retail-related jobs. For six weeks, these trainees spend part of the day in the classroom learning retail skills, such as operating a cash register, and the remainder of the day working in the Goodwill Industries store with Anne's supportive presence. During the next six weeks of their training, the trainees work in satellite Goodwill stores with less support, thus preparing them for the competitive world.

Anne finds her work rewarding because she can see that she is directly helping people. For example, a formerly institutionalized mental patient is now working full-time in a shoe store. A woman with multiple personality disorder is employed part-time in a discount store. Many of Anne's former trainees who are grateful to be self-sufficient send her cards and homemade gifts to thank her for her help. Goodwill Industries has many jobs like Anne's that let Good Samaritans and humanitarians help job trainees. Job placement specialists find jobs for the trainees and then work with them on their new jobs. There are also case management workers.

This is Anne's first professional job. She became acquainted with Goodwill Industries by working there as an intern. After graduating with a bachelor of science degree in vocational rehabilitation, she obtained a paid position with the organization. Anne also has teaching credentials. To become a more effective training coordinator, she is currently working toward obtaining a work experience handicapped license. In the future, Anne believes she would like to help even younger people; she is considering going into high school guidance and counseling.

Boy Scouts of America

It is the mission of the Boy Scouts to serve others by helping to instill values in young people and, in other ways, to prepare them to make ethical choices over their lifetime in achieving their full potential. The Boy Scout movement was founded in Great Britain in 1907. A chance meeting in a London fog between a lost Chicago businessman and a British Boy Scout who helped him find his way led to the founding of a similar organization, the Boy Scouts of America, in 1910 by William D. Boyce.

Unlike some other social service organizations, the Boy Scouts promotes from within. To be considered for an entry-level professional position, a bachelor's degree is required. While work experience is an asset, it is not a prerequisite to working for the Scouts. Most professionals start as district executives, who are responsible for all the scouting activities in a designated geographical area. The district executive recruits, guides, trains, motivates, and inspires all the volunteer leaders. Initial pay starts at about $25,000; district executives are also given a car. Future pay varies, because the Scouts is a merit-pay organization.

After three years, the district executive can expect to be promoted to a larger district or to start supervising entry-level personnel. The next step, four or five years later, is to a field position managing district executives or into a support program in an area such as finance, fund-raising, or directing programs. Through classes at the regional and national levels, professionals receive training that prepares them for advancement in the organization.

Mark Holtz's life has been devoted to the Boy Scouts. He was a Cub Scout and Eagle Scout, he worked at a Scout camp during the summers while he was in college, and he has been employed in the Scouts organization full-time for the past fourteen years. After completing his bachelor's degree, Mark became a district executive and then climbed through the ranks to become director of field services and then executive of a council. He plans to continue to work in scouting.

Mark's career satisfaction comes from seeing the good his organization is doing for boys and the impact scouting has had on individual lives. While he was a district executive, he organized a troop for learning-delayed boys. One of these boys has gone on to work in a fast-food restaurant, participate in a state Special

Olympics meet, and attend Scout summer camp. In a magazine article about what her son has accomplished, the boy's mother gave special thanks to the Scout leaders who saw the needs and potential of handicapped people and had the conviction that all boys should have the chance to be Scouts.

CARE: Cooperative for American Relief Everywhere

You may know CARE as the organization that has sent one hundred million "CARE packages" to needy people, beginning with victims of World War II in Europe and Asia. Now CARE sends experts to work with people in Africa, Asia, Latin America, Eastern Europe, and the former Soviet Union to help the developing world's poor strive for social and economic well-being. While the scope of CARE's work is broad, its vision focuses on a single concept: helping people help themselves. This means training health workers, immunizing children, providing loans to small businesses, helping villages plant trees, enabling poor farmers to grow more food, building roads and water systems, and rushing aid to the scene when disasters strike. In short, CARE meets the needs— immediate and long-term—of the world's neediest people.

CARE is one of the world's largest nonprofit, nonsectarian, independent relief and development organizations. In 2004, it provided direct benefits to forty-five million people in seventy countries. In the United States, the plight of the poor and homeless is certainly severe. But there are government programs and social service organizations working to meet the needs of these people, providing some options in difficult times. In developing countries, these options rarely exist. Organizations like CARE are often the only help for developing countries.

CARE was founded in 1945 when twenty-two American organizations joined together to help World War II survivors. CARE's history includes airlifting food to Berlin, training Peace Corps volunteers, and being the first private development organization to work in the People's Republic of China. Today, CARE has programs in agriculture and natural resources; control of HIV/AIDS and other sexually transmitted diseases; emergency assistance; health, food, and nutrition; population and reproductive health; economic activity development; and water and sanitation.

Humanitarian Jobs: Highly Sought. At first glance, you might assume that Lisa Nichols is an investment banker or a hard-driving entrepreneur. She's young, well groomed, and obsessed with her work. On the job up to eighty hours a week, she calls her work "the most important thing" in her life. She met all of her current friends at work, but she is not a Wall Street workaholic with a million-dollar income and an ulcer. Lisa works for CARE in the West African country of Mali. Her neighbors in the flat, treeless land on the southern rim of the Sahara are among the poorest people in the world. Her tiny three-room house on the outskirts of the town of Bamako has no air conditioning or indoor plumbing. "My job isn't glamorous, and it will never make me rich, but I love the challenge of it," says Lisa, who manages healthcare services for 250 Malian villages for CARE. "I'm glad that what I do helps people, even saves their lives, but I don't think of myself as exceptional."

Lisa is an example of a whole new breed of professionals called relief and development specialists. These Good Samaritans and humanitarians are not starry-eyed do-gooders, but rather experts in helping the world's desperately poor people find permanent solutions to hunger and poverty. Lisa had plenty of competitors for her job in Mali, despite occupational hazards that include blinding sandstorms and 120-degree heat.

CARE currently receives a minimum of two hundred resumes a week from experienced people who usually have postgraduate degrees, two to three years' professional experience in the developing world, and the requisite foreign language requirements. Those who succeed at this work demonstrate the same business acumen, personal diplomacy, and basic toughness that many corporations seek in an employee. For example, during the famine in

Mali, Lisa managed a CARE truck fleet that was hauling grain. It wasn't easy for Lisa to work shoulder-to-shoulder with the male drivers in a Muslim country where women do not give orders to men, but eventually she and the men became a solid team.

Lisa has made impoverished women and their children her focus, spearheading innovative projects in such distant locales as Bangladesh and Mali. Today, Lisa trains women in prenatal nutrition, hygiene, sanitation, and the importance of immunizations. These women then pass the information along to their neighbors. Lisa's goal is not to fix every problem herself but to pass along the skills that people need to fix problems themselves. This philosophy has won her the respect and affection of the local Malians. When her mother visited Lisa in Mali, she immediately saw this. The people were always giving Lisa and her mother food and gifts. And when they arrived at a village, the children would run along beside their truck, happily shouting "Lisa! Lisa!"

The American Red Cross

Whenever disaster strikes—whether it is a hurricane, a flood, an earthquake, or a fire in a home—the American Red Cross is there, helping victims. Disaster relief may be the service you most closely identify with the organization that flies the familiar flag of a red cross on a white background, but the Red Cross also offers many other humanitarian services. Instructors teach health and safety courses to give people the knowledge and skills to save and improve lives. They offer courses in CPR, first aid, water safety, child safety, parenting skills, and HIV/AIDS information.

For members of the armed forces, their families, and veterans, the Red Cross offers emergency communication, help in coping with emergencies, a referral service to help cut through red tape, assistance in requesting humanitarian reassignment, and more.

The Red Cross's blood program collects and distributes more than half of the donated blood in this country and maintains a registry of volunteer donors of rare blood types. The Red Cross also offers transplant services for heart valves and bone and skin tissue products to those with disabling conditions. And there are many other Red Cross services to meet the needs of people in almost every community in the United States.

The Red Cross has nearly thirty thousand paid staff members and 1.3 million volunteers working through more than thirteen hundred local chapters to implement its vast array of services. Each chapter has access to the resources of the national Red Cross organization; it is also linked to the International Red Cross so that a number of international services can be offered.

Since the formation of the American Red Cross in 1881 by Clara Barton and others, the organization has always adapted its services to meet current community needs. Within this huge organization, Good Samaritans and humanitarians can find jobs helping people in their own communities and around the world.

Red Cross Volunteer. Terri Garcia began volunteering with the Red Cross after her children entered high school and she found herself with more free time. Terri became interested in the Red Cross after a family friend approached her about volunteering some of her free time. Terri assisted in organizing the national conference several years ago and enjoys spending time with an organization that is neutral and worldwide. Terri was asked to join the board of directors in 2001 and is now chair of the youth committee. She spends much of her time working with several local school systems to set up a mentoring program, Together We Can Prepare.

Caseworker for Emergency Services. Mike Booth's job involves helping people deal with emergencies. He is not personally on the scene of every local disaster, but he makes sure that someone—usually a volunteer—from the Red Cross is. For example, when fire destroys a home, Mike must see that the family's emergency needs are met. This involves finding a place for the family to stay and providing the absolute necessities until the family has found shelter again.

Mike's job extends to the international arena, too. He helps reunite families that are out of touch because of war or natural disaster, such as Ethiopian refugees in Sudan seeking relatives in the United States so the refugees can come to this country. Mike also sees that emergency messages are transmitted for military families. Mike has left the local chapter for three-week stints to join Red Cross teams providing care and food services to disaster victims in Puerto Rico, Arkansas, Texas, and Wisconsin.

Mike has always been a hands-on helper of people. Before coming to the Red Cross, he was a caseworker at an emergency shelter and a financial technician for his county, providing emergency money for people who were evicted or needed medical treatment. Mike's future plans include earning a master's degree so he will have the knowledge and tools to hold a position in which he can make more decisions. He plans to stay at the Red Cross because he likes the fact that he can do a variety of jobs and help different groups of people.

Caseworker with Several Responsibilities. Julie Hankins believes that she has found the perfect job for a caring person as a caseworker in a Red Cross unit that serves a four-county area. On the job, she has three major responsibilities. She wears a beeper all the time and responds to calls to the Red Cross in case of disasters, which could mean a fire at an apartment house, a plane crash, or a devastating ice storm such as the one that immobilized the area in 1995. Often, Julie has to get a team of volunteers together and hurry to the scene of the disaster, where she may provide nourishment from the disaster van, assist people in finding housing, or comfort distraught individuals.

Another part of Julie's job is helping members of the military and their families stay in touch. She knows that time is of the essence, for example, when it comes to getting a soldier or sailor home to say good-bye to a dying family member. Julie frequently speaks to members of the military in her community, letting them know how the Red Cross can help them. Besides disaster relief and military work, this busy caseworker is also the director of the 450 volunteers who help out with the work of her chapter. In this role, she is involved in recruiting and interviewing volunteers and giving a lot of orientation. Julie loves her job because it gives her a chance to make a difference in others' lives.

Volunteers of America

Volunteers of America was founded in 1896 by Ballington Booth, the second son of the founder of the Salvation Army, and his wife, Maud. This large, nonprofit, Christian social service organization is a pioneer in implementing humanitarian objectives with action programs. In the beginning, the Volunteers of America concentrated on relieving poverty in slums and rehabilitating skid row derelicts and former convicts living in New York City. Although such efforts still have a high priority, today's expanded range of services reflects the organization's involvement in contemporary problems at all economic and social levels of society. Throughout the country, in more than 160 different programs, the services of the Volunteers of America include:

- day-care centers
- family centers providing health care
- group homes for mentally and physically disabled persons
- halfway houses for rehabilitating alcohol and other drug abusers
- long-term care facilities
- missions for the homeless
- nonprofit housing complexes
- prerelease centers preparing paroled prisoners for their reentry into society
- senior citizen centers with health clinics and recreational programs
- senior nutrition programs
- shelters for adolescent runaways
- vocational guidance and personal counseling

The staff of the Volunteers of America is made up of individuals who not only have administrative and/or professional social work expertise, but who also have a commitment to the Christian mission of the organization—the reaching and uplifting of all people.

Bar-None Residential Treatment Center Therapist. The Bar-None Residential Treatment Center, a Volunteers of America facility, is located on 710 acres of woods, pastures, and lakes in Minnesota. For twenty-five years, Larry Weight has worked at Bar-None, helping youths who are emotionally or behaviorally disturbed. It is unusual for a therapist to remain at one facility for such a long time, because staying with one treatment center can often limit the therapist's focus. But this hasn't happened to Larry because at Bar-None, staff members are periodically asked what they want to do next and then challenged to do it.

This job flexibility is part of the work at Bar-None because the mission of the Volunteers of America includes meeting unmet needs. So, over the years, the professional staff at Bar-None has had the opportunity to discover their unmet needs and develop programs to satisfy them. This has given Larry the chance to work with different populations and be part of a team that created a program for children with autism and those with autistic-like characteristics—one of his special interests.

Today, Larry is director of clinical services, and he supervises treatment in all programs at Bar-None. But beyond his administrative duties, he is usually involved with counseling one or two youths, a family, or a group. Larry's professional background includes a bachelor's degree in social work as well as graduate courses. He is a licensed clinical social worker. His professional satisfaction lies in being part of an agency where he can be creative in working with disturbed youths.

The Jailer Who Gets Thank-You Notes. Inmates actually write to Bill Nelson to thank him for the uplifting experience that jail has been for them. Bill is the director at the Regional Corrections Center, a jail, workhouse, and work-release program for women that allows them to be placed in a community setting rather than a state or federal jail. This facility, run by the Volunteers of America, has all the trappings of a jail—security, searches, and head counts. But this is a new-generation jail, where there is no physical separation between guards, known as shift managers, and inmates. The shift managers get their power from the professional relationship established with the inmates. And there is a different philosophy here, too. People don't come to this jail to be punished but rather to be uplifted—to be exposed to a different, more rewarding lifestyle.

The inmates' time is filled with ballet classes, yoga instruction, vocational training, counseling, and learning to take control of their bodies and emotions. The thank-you letters from the inmates to "Mr. Bill," as they affectionately call Bill Nelson, attest that his commitment to the Volunteers of America's mission of uplifting people has produced a jail that actually helps people change their lifestyles.

The story of this Good Samaritan is not limited to his success with the Regional Corrections Center. Bill is also responsible for the success of a halfway house. Twenty-five years ago, nine thousand neighbors protested against having this halfway house, for men returning to the community from prison, in their neighborhood. Today, up to 150 neighbors come to self-help programs at this same house each week. In addition, Bill and the staff of the halfway house put on a weekly television show to talk to the public about selected aspects of the criminal justice system.

With a background of degrees in sociology and social work, plus ten years of experience in correctional agencies, Bill began to work for Volunteers of America twenty-three years ago. He credits his success in helping others to a combination of organization, a commitment to thoroughness, unshakable optimism, and the freedom the Volunteers of America has given him to come up with creative ideas. Bill is now starting on a major community project to work effectively with women and children involved in prostitution. One of the program's initiatives will be to create transitional housing and services for individuals wishing to leave the prostitution lifestyle. Bill's work exemplifies how a career as a Good Samaritan can touch the lives of people with very different needs.

Horizon House

Horizon House is the focal point for homeless individuals to access services in Indianapolis, Indiana. This resource center and day center was designed to be a one-stop-shop for homeless individuals to access basic needs services and a variety of professional services. Case managers at Horizon House assist individuals with mental illnesses, addictions, lack of education, and many other barriers.

Being the Missing Link. Linking homeless individuals to appropriate resources in the community, advocating for their needs and rights, and counseling them to make changes in their lives are the responsibilities of the case managers at Horizon House. Melissa Marquardt spends much of her time listening to her clients and determining a plan to end their homelessness, which they commit to following through with. Melissa likes to identify the strengths and talents that each client possesses and determine how these strengths can be utilized to end the client's homelessness.

Volunteers. Volunteers keep Horizon House functioning. AmeriCorps*State and AmeriCorps*VISTA members commit a year of their life to assist in building capacity through increasing funding and agency programs. Volunteers who work in various capacities throughout the agency are a vital part of the daily operation of the day center. Volunteers assist individuals who are seeking employment by helping them develop their resumes and have positive interactions with individuals utilizing services and by organizing donations. Volunteers make a positive and significant impact on the homeless individuals in Indianapolis.

Project for Pride in Living

Decent, affordable housing is unattainable for many people. Since 1972, Project for Pride in Living (PPL) has been housing inner-city residents by building or rehabilitating houses and apartments to sell or rent at affordable prices. This organization, which was started with a $200 grant from the Pillsbury Company, is now one of the largest Twin Cities landlords for the poor.

The driving force behind the establishment and operation of PPL is Joe Selvaggio, a former priest, who was the organization's executive director for many years and now devotes his time to raising funds. Over the years, PPL has developed programs that link social services and job skills training with housing and that provide housing-related services to improve aging neighborhoods. In spite of how the organization has grown, from one person to a staff of about seventy-five full-time and about two hundred job-training positions, the goal remains the same: helping people to help themselves.

PPL Self-Sufficiency Program. The PPL Self-Sufficiency Program (SSP) is designed to help the people in PPL rental units and training programs overcome self-sufficiency barriers and gain control of their lives. Services include one-on-one counseling, goal setting, resume writing, interview practice, employment and child-care referrals, educational tutoring, support groups and retreats, transportation, advocacy, assistance in locating furnishings, and financial assistance for tuition and child care. What this means on a daily basis for the staff is interacting very closely with the people who seek their help. The counselors know the program's participants and the participants' children well.

Job satisfaction is high because results are visible. Staff members see participants who now pay their rent on time, who have acquired jobs or advanced in their current jobs, and who are in educational programs or training to improve their work skills.

Susan Baldwin began her work at PPL as the manager of the SSP program. She started her career as a corporate librarian, but the job simply didn't feel right to Susan. She wanted to connect with people, and she began working as a volunteer with battered women. Susan went back to school and designed her own major in social communications and counseling, with emphasis on women's issues, while working as a librarian and a volunteer.

Susan's first job after she received her degree was starting a transitional living program for battered women. The job was so enjoyable that Susan almost couldn't believe she was being paid. She is convinced that it was her volunteer experience more than her new degree that helped her get this position. Two years later, Susan moved to the Twin Cities and learned about her next job, as a lead family specialist at the YWCA, through someone working there.

Today, Susan is director of human services and administration, running the office as well as the volunteer program, child-care initiative, and a welfare-to-work program. One of her responsibilities is hiring staff. Like every other member of her staff, Susan had completed a master's degree in counseling and psychological services. However, she looks at experience (volunteering counts) as more important than college degrees and believes talking face-to-face is more effective for the job seeker than just relying on a resume. Resumes, she feels, don't truly indicate the job seeker's commitment or compassion for others.

Citizens Council Victim Services

Strong feelings of anger, powerlessness, shame, and fear are normal reactions to being the victim of a crime. Unfortunately, many victims of misdemeanor crimes do not know what their legal rights are. The staff and volunteers of a unique organization, Citizens Council Victim Services, provide crisis-intervention counseling and act as advocates in court for victims of crimes. Victims do have the right to speak at sentencings, and the staff and volunteers help them handle the court procedures.

Crime victim specialists who answer the crisis line find that crime victims often question how they have responded to a situation. The specialists help victims to critically examine what happened, stressing that they have survived, and, when appropriate, they discuss ways to avoid a repetition of the crime. For example, a handicapped woman, nearly hysterical because she had been robbed after leaving a convenience store, regretted that she had not hit her attacker with her crutches. A crime victim specialist was able to calm her and help her realize that she had, in fact, handled the situation well. The specialist took steps to ensure that the woman had groceries, since so much of her money for the month had been stolen, and, because it was Thanksgiving, even made sure she had a turkey. All of the crime victim specialists find great satisfaction in devising creative solutions to help crime victims.

Children's Bureau

The Children's Bureau in Indianapolis supports and assists children and families that are at risk by developing healthy families for each child through various programs, including adoption services, home-based counseling, parent education, group homes, transitional living, and case management services. The Children's Bureau has grown over the years since its conception and now employs more than two hundred individuals.

Stopping Abuse Before It Starts. Amy Johnson is a case manager for Children's Bureau's Any Child program, which works with families that are at risk for child abuse and neglect. Any Child's goal is to keep these families from becoming involved with Child Protective Services. Amy works with the families on parenting skills, stress management, child development, and other needs the family might present. Amy identifies and connects families to resources in the community and does whatever is necessary to help the family unit thrive and be self-sufficient.

Planning Your Career

People often fantasize about working in Africa, Central America, Appalachia, or New York City, ministering to the hungry, hopeless, or homeless. Altruistic dreams of serving others by doing good works are to be admired, but not everyone has the commitment, education, or experience to match their dreams. If you believe that a career being a Good Samaritan or humanitarian in a social service organization is right for you, check it out early by working as a volunteer while in high school or college. Then get an education that will give you the expertise to function effectively in your chosen career. This usually means getting a bachelor's degree to secure your first job and a master's degree early in your career to give you the additional skills necessary for career advancement. For a bird's-eye view of a specific social service career, job shadow by spending several hours with a professional at the workplace.

Selecting the organization where you want to work can be a mind-boggling task since there are more than four thousand social service organizations. In making this decision, it is helpful to consider your preferences, such as working with:

- a small, medium, or large organization
- a single-service or multiservice organization
- a domestic or overseas job
- a specific or more general population

You will also want to learn more about the social service organizations that may have the perfect job for you. Review the list of job search tools given in Chapter 1, and be sure to look at the United Way community resources directory to become familiar with local organizations. For information about international humanitarian efforts, see Appendix A.

CHAPTER THREE

Caring for People Around the World Through Government Work

"We make a living by what we get. We make a life by what we give."
—Winston Churchill

Homelessness, hunger, poor health, illiteracy, crime, and abuse are serious problems found in the United States and around the world. Good Samaritans and humanitarians can find many career opportunities that address these issues through government agencies working to end these problems. The federal, state, and local governments in the United States as well as the United Nations and other international bodies have all initiated welfare, relief, and development programs to make a dent in the problems that poverty brings.

The government hasn't always played a role in helping the poor. At one time, families, neighbors, and the church took responsibility for helping the needy. Only in 1601, when the English Parliament passed the Act for the Relief of the Poor, did a government first take steps to provide for the poor. This act required local government units to levy taxes to support the poor in their jurisdictions. Poorhouses were established so that the poor had shelter, but they also had to work in order to pay for their keep.

Conditions in most of these poorhouses were so dreadful that the poor avoided seeking help from them.

In the early years of U.S. history, the way the poor were treated was much the same as in Great Britain because the two countries had similar welfare legislation. By the early 1900s, however, many of the states had initiated welfare legislation requiring cities and counties to help the aged, the blind, and fatherless children. States even paid some of the costs of those programs. During the Great Depression, the federal government became active in helping the poor, as a result of Franklin Roosevelt's New Deal legislation. And in 1945, with the founding of the United Nations, there was finally an international organization that provided help for the poor throughout the world.

At all levels of government in the United States today, there is a strong commitment to helping needy people—from newborn infants to elderly citizens. And this commitment means a great number of government jobs for Good Samaritans and humanitarians. At the federal level, these jobs tend to be administrative in nature, because it is here that programs to help the needy are planned, developed, and supervised. It is at the city, county, and state levels that most hands-on work is found. Because programs to help the needy are under different jurisdictions in individual states, you could find yourself doing the same job for a city, county, or state governmental unit, depending on where you live. For example, in Minnesota most social workers are county employees, while in Illinois they are state employees. By studying state guidebooks of services and visiting state, county, and city government employment offices, you can determine which governmental unit in your state has the most appropriate jobs for Good Samaritans and humanitarians.

Government Jobs at the Federal Level

The federal government offers rewarding and interesting jobs that let Good Samaritans and humanitarians serve people in an incredible number of areas. Because this job arena is so large, job seekers must learn which agencies are most likely to have jobs for people who want to help others. One way to do this is by studying the latest edition of *The United States Government Manual*, published by the Office of the Federal Register and available in most public libraries or searchable online at www.gpoaccess.gov/gmanual. The manual gives information on the agencies of each branch of the government as well as quasi-official agencies and international organizations in which the United States participates. A typical agency description includes a brief history, descriptions of its programs and activities, and phone numbers for more information. You will find similar information in *The Directory of Federal Jobs and Employers* by Ronald L. Krannich and Caryl Rae Krannich. *Government Job Finder* by Daniel Lauber not only tells you where government jobs can be found, but it also gives job hotline numbers and the website addresses of new online job services.

One-third of all federal government employees work in Washington, D.C. However, having a job with the federal government does not necessarily mean working in the nation's capital; there are many jobs in regional offices, cities, counties, and states where federal programs are actually carried out.

You can find out about job vacancies by visiting state employment offices and Federal Job Information Centers, calling agency job hotline phone numbers, attending government job fairs, and reading ads in newspapers and professional journals. Be sure to look at *Federal Jobs Digest* (www.jobsfed.com), published by Breakthrough Publications. This digest lists thousands of job vacancies in agencies throughout the country and gives application addresses for each vacancy. This biweekly publication can be found in public libraries. You can also visit FedWorld, a program of the U.S. Department of Commerce, online at www.fedworld.gov to learn about federal job opportunities.

Although getting a job with the federal government is not quite as complicated or lengthy a process as it once was, most applicants will profit from reading a book like *Find a Federal Job Fast* by Ronald L. Krannich and Caryl Rae Krannich, which explains the hiring process. It is also wise to learn more about communicating your qualifications on the standard form used by most agencies. *The Right SF-171 Writer* by Russ Smith will help you in this task.

The typical procedure for getting a federal job starts with completing an application for a position. Next, a score is determined based on a written test, a training and experience rating, or an oral examination. Then your name is placed on a list used to fill vacancies as they arise.

Three Agencies with Jobs for Good Samaritans and Humanitarians

Although there are many agencies that help those in need, the Department of Health and Human Services (HHS) touches the lives of more of the needy than any other federal agency. HHS serves people through familiar divisions such as the Social Security Administration and the Public Health Service, as well as the less familiar Health Care Financing Administration, the Office of Human Development Services, and the Family Support Administration.

Another federal agency that Good Samaritans and humanitarians should investigate is the Federal Emergency Management Agency (FEMA), which prepares for and responds to the full range of emergencies—natural, technological, and attack-related. Its activities include hazard mitigation, preparedness planning, relief operations, and recovery assistance.

Because the Veterans Administration (VA) operates diverse programs to benefit veterans and their families, it also has jobs for Good Samaritans and humanitarians. These jobs are mainly in the areas of education and rehabilitation and medical treatment.

United States Agency for International Development (USAID)

A job with USAID allows Good Samaritans and humanitarians to help with efforts to reduce poverty, ignorance, and malnutrition in developing countries. Since 1961, this agency has carried out economic assistance programs designed to help third world countries maintain their own health-care systems and provide food, clothing, and jobs for their people. In Egypt, school enrollment has increased 13 percent because USAID has built more than five hundred schools there since 1975. In India, USAID-sponsored research has led to the development of hybrid crops capable of adapting to adverse weather conditions. A USAID nutrition education program in Morocco resulted in a 69 percent reduction in moderate and severe malnutrition. Millions of entrepreneurs around the world (many of them women) have started or improved small businesses through USAID assistance.

USAID projects require people with highly specialized talents—just having humanitarian impulses won't get the job done. For this reason, the Agency initiated the International Development Intern (IDI) Program in 1968. The IDI program is USAID's entry-level program into the Foreign Service and seeks the best-qualified junior professional candidates who are willing to make a long-term career commitment to the Foreign Service and international development. IDIs begin their careers in formal training programs that are followed by rotational on-the-job, Washington-based training for up to one year. After completion of Washington training, IDIs are assigned to overseas missions and receive broad-based training through rotational assignments. The total IDI training time is approximately three years.

To apply for the IDI program and to view open positions, visit the U.S. Agency for International Development's website at www.usaid.gov.

An IDI Graduate's Story. David Grossman possessed the qualifications needed for selection to the IDI program. He earned a graduate degree from the School of International Affairs at Columbia University, had worked for the United Nations, and spoke fluent Spanish. After training in Washington, D.C., and Honduras, David remained in Honduras in a staff position. Then he was assigned to Costa Rica as a general development manager. This assignment related closely to an interest David had in urban development as a graduate student.

For four years, David remained in Costa Rica, designing and implementing projects that had very visible results. People who had been living in cardboard shacks were able to move to their own modest brick homes because of the program to finance lower-income homes. Women from low-income areas learned how to sew and then found jobs because of the vocational training program. Small businesses were able to grow because they obtained needed machinery or supplies with loans from the small business credit program.

Upon completion of his overseas assignments, David returned to Washington, D.C., to work in USAID's Office of Housing and Urban Programs as the assistant director for the Program Support division. When the agency was reorganized to consolidate technical groups in a global bureau, David became a program officer for the Environment Center. Now he is working not only to help people but to improve the planet for everyone. Reflecting upon his career with USAID, David asks, "What could be more rewarding than helping people while being stimulated by the challenge of improving the global environment?"

A Long-Term USAID Employee. Influenced by the idealism of the Kennedy era, John Fasullo joined the Peace Corps after graduation from college in large part because he wanted to contribute to the pursuit of a better life for the less fortunate. For John, it certainly was a bigger challenge than selling stocks, bonds, or insurance.

After the Peace Corps, John enjoyed a brief assignment as a forest ranger before being selected to go to Vietnam as his first assignment with USAID. At the start of his Vietnam assignment, he was loaned to the Stanford Research Institute to work on land reform in the delta. When the 1968 Tet offensive made the continuation of this work impossible, he returned to USAID and worked as a regional youth advisor, helping young Vietnamese develop youth programs.

John saw his work in Vietnam as an extension of his work with the Peace Corps in that he was there to assist the Vietnamese with their overall development, especially as it related to the rural sector. Subsequently, he was accepted into the IDI program, spending most of his two years as an intern in Lima, Peru, where he was exposed to the major components of the USAID program.

Back in Washington, D.C., for four years, John worked in the office of management planning. In 1976 he began his next overseas assignment in Costa Rica, where he worked with Costa Rican research and extension agencies to enhance agricultural production for almost five years. Like John, most USAID Foreign Service officers spend the majority of their careers overseas.

John then returned to the United States in 1981 to gain needed technical academic experience in rural development and international agriculture. After a year at Cornell University, John was assigned by USAID to Bolivia for almost seven years. For part of that time, he oversaw a regional development project in the Chapare, a region southeast of La Paz where 90 percent of the coca that is grown finds its way into the illegal narcotics market. This project attempted to change the agricultural habits of generations of farmers accustomed to growing coca—a very lucrative crop. USAID provided assistance to the government of Bolivia in the areas of infrastructure development, including road maintenance, accessing electricity, the provision of credit, and research on alternative crops as an inducement to stop the farmers from growing coca and then as a benefit to those who had reduced their acreage of coca. Before John left Bolivia for an assignment in Washington, D.C., he was pleased to see the crop substitution program of USAID showing some signs of working.

The Peace Corps

The recruitment slogan for the Peace Corps is "the toughest job you'll ever love." It's an appropriate description, for Peace Corps assignments are tough, demanding, sometimes frustrating, and always rewarding. Today, approximately seventy-seven hundred volunteers are working in almost seventy-two countries, showing how America cares person-to-person. In Guatemala, for example, volunteers are helping Guatemalans to increase off-farm income and manage and conserve natural resources. In Nepal, volunteers are teaching English and science in primary and secondary schools. And in Mozambique, where the illiteracy rate is 40 percent, they are focusing their attention on establishing schools and teaching at the secondary level.

Since the creation of the Peace Corps on March 1, 1961, by an executive order of President John F. Kennedy, almost 178,000 volunteers have shared their skills and energies with people in developing countries. After completing a training program, volunteers work for two years. Expenses for housing, food, and utilities may be paid by the host agency of a country or by the volunteers out of their living allowance. Upon completion of their assignments, volunteers are paid about $6,000 to cover costs of transitioning back into life at home.

Qualifications. To qualify for the Peace Corps, you must be a United States citizen, eighteen years of age or older (few people younger than twenty-one actually qualify), and in good health. You must also have an appropriate skill, which means having either a few years of work experience in a selected area—such as forestry, farming, nursing, teaching, or carpentry—or a college degree with units in certain courses and/or experience in extracurricular activities. While the need has remained for volunteers to work in agriculture, education, forestry, health, engineering, and skilled trades, countries are increasingly requesting help in new areas: business, the environment, urban planning, youth development, and the teaching of English for commerce and technology.

Selection. Applications for the Peace Corps can take up to nine months to process, and applicants need to be available to take up their assignments within one year after submitting the forms. Selection for a Peace Corps assignment involves completing an application form, being interviewed by a Peace Corps recruiter, and having the skills requested by host countries for particular programs. Successful applicants are invited to enter a training program and, upon successful completion of the training, are selected as Peace Corps volunteers.

Information about and applications for the Peace Corps are available from regional offices. These offices also handle recruiting. It is also possible to get information and to download an application from the Peace Corps website at www.peacecorps.gov.

Training. Peace Corps training sessions last about three months and are usually held in host countries. An in-depth orientation to the culture and traditions of the host country and to personal health and safety issues is given. Technical training is also provided to help volunteers adapt their skills to their overseas assignments. Since volunteers are expected to speak the language of the people with whom they will live and work, language instruction is usually quite intense during training.

A Volunteer in Cameroon. Karen Smith was selected by the Peace Corps to teach English in Cameroon. This country is located on the western coast of central Africa and is slightly larger than California. In Cameroon, the national language of commerce is English; however, the language used in the schools is French, and most children speak a tribal language before entering school.

Karen's introduction to the Peace Corps began with a seven-day orientation program in Philadelphia with fifty other volunteers. Then the group spent nearly three months training in Cameroon. During training, the volunteers lived in a dormitory in a mission and had all their domestic needs taken care of so they could concentrate on academics. Classes were held eight hours a day, six days a week. Besides being immersed in French language classes, Karen, who graduated from college with a degree in history, also spent time preparing lessons and doing practice teaching in a model school the Peace Corps set up.

When the training period was over, Karen was sent to Garoua-Boulai, a small, dusty town with one main street, to teach English in the public junior high school. Karen's home was probably the best house in the town. It was a cement home with a tin roof; it had plumbing fixtures but no running water. Karen was the only Peace Corps volunteer in the town, but it wasn't a lonely experience because she became good friends with a Cameroonian family living across the street, and she ate most of her meals with them.

At the school, Karen had to make the most of limited supplies. But teaching a language offers opportunities for imaginative learning experiences through dialogues and plays, so not having materials was not an insurmountable problem. Although she wasn't a trained teacher, Karen felt comfortable at this job because of the excellent preparation during the training program. The language proficiency her students demonstrated was gratifying, but much of what made her experience memorable was being adopted by the community and learning about their culture. She hopes to share her culture with the family who befriended her in Garoua-Boulai by sponsoring their children in school in the United States when they are older.

AmeriCorps—the National Service Program

AmeriCorps is a new national service initiative with the goal of getting things done. It involves people in programs designed to strengthen individuals and communities. AmeriCorps members serve throughout the United States in hundreds of local programs. AmeriCorps includes two national programs: AmeriCorps* NCCC (National Civilian Community Corps) and Ameri-Corps*VISTA (Volunteers in Service to America). NCCC is a full-time residential program for members from eighteen to twenty-four years of age. They work in teams and live together in housing complexes. Their efforts are focused on the environment, education, public safety, unmet human needs, and disaster relief assistance. You can find out more about both programs by visiting the website at www.americorps.gov.

VISTA: Volunteers in Service to America. You don't have to travel the globe to find a challenge. Three years after the Peace Corps was established to help people in other countries, VISTA was created by Congress to give idealistic Americans an opportunity to meet the needs of people at their doorstep by working full-time with locally sponsored projects.

Six thousand VISTA volunteers are assigned to nonprofit organizations to combat illiteracy, improve health services, create businesses, increase housing opportunities, and bridge the digital divide. The volunteers live and work among the poor, serving in urban and rural areas, helping the agency provide opportunities for low-income people to improve the condition of their lives and communities. A VISTA project is considered successful when the work continues after the volunteers have left.

To be a VISTA volunteer, you must be a citizen, national, or resident alien and at least eighteen years old. VISTA volunteers serve for one year. During that time, they receive a monthly subsistence allowance equivalent to the cost of living in the low-income community where they are serving. They also receive health-care coverage and deferment of any previous school loans. After their assignment is completed, they have the option of receiving either an education voucher worth $4,725 that can be applied toward past loans or schooling within seven years, or a stipend of $100 for each month of service.

VISTA volunteers in Indiana, for example, cover a broad spectrum of needs in their communities. Volunteers focus on asset development, family strengthening, homelessness, homeland security, prison re-entry, service learning, and older Americans. Members gain experience with grant writing, fund-raising, volunteer recruitment, and program development, to name just a few.

Caroline Richardson spent her term of service building the capacity of a homeless service agency by researching and identifying new funding sources and writing grants. Caroline was also able to participate in numerous trainings, fund-raisers, and committees that assisted her in developing skills to help in future employment.

Annette Vazquez spent her time of service working on building the capacity of a literacy program focused on serving homeless individuals reading below the sixth grade reading level. She assisted with fund-raising, volunteer recruitment, and grant writing. These experiences were a huge learning experience for Annette, since she came from an art background. VISTA offers individuals the great opportunity to serve their communities as well as develop skills that they can use to be Good Samaritans and humanitarians in the future.

Two Presidents Speak About VISTA. President Lyndon Johnson concluded his speech to the first group of VISTA volunteers by saying, "Your pay will be low; the conditions of your labor often will be difficult. But you will have the satisfaction of leading a great national effort, and you will have the ultimate reward which comes to those who serve their fellow man."

On January 31, 1990, President Bush spoke to current and new VISTA volunteers on the twenty-fifth anniversary of the organization. He described the mission given to VISTA by President Johnson—"to guide the young, to comfort the sick, to encourage the downtrodden, to teach the skills which may lead to a more rewarding life." Then he went on to say, "That was your mission then and that certainly is your mission today. Every time a kid learns to read, you make a difference. Every time a homeless family finds shelter, you make a difference. And every time a troubled person stays off drugs, you make a difference for all Americans. . . . Sounds like a miracle. Maybe it is. It is a miracle that comes from caring."

Government Jobs at the State Level

In all state governments, there are a great number of agencies devoted to helping needy adults and children. Many of the people employed in these agencies plan, administer, and coordinate programs rather than work with people, because the programs themselves are actually operated by counties or cities. Within every state, however, Good Samaritans and humanitarians can find jobs dealing directly with people.

A particularly good place to look for jobs is the Department of Human Services, also called Public Welfare, which often is the largest agency in a state. Good Samaritans may be attracted to working in this agency as behavior analysts, human rights enforcement officers, occupational therapists, psychologists, and social workers. Within economic security agencies, you will find positions as rehabilitation counselors and job and training representatives. In corrections, employees are needed to supervise and counsel adults and juveniles on probation or parole as well as prison inmates.

To find out what jobs are available in your state, call the job information line. Listen to the recording that describes job responsibilities, hiring processes, salary ranges, locations, and test requirements for current job openings. To find out more about available jobs, go to state job service offices or to individual state agencies. Many states have listed employment opportunities online. Visit their websites and look for links such as "Employment," "Human Resources," and "Personnel."

For most state jobs, you must pass a civil service exam. These exams are either experience and training ratings or written tests. Experience and training ratings are evaluations of your work experience and education as they relate to the requirements of the job you are seeking. You receive a score based on the information given on your job application. Written tests are usually multiple-choice and are based on job-related subjects.

Once you have passed a civil service exam, your name is put on a list of eligible candidates. When a state agency has a job opening, the names of a certain number of people with the highest scores on the list are sent to the agency. Obviously, the higher your score, the better your opportunity to be referred to an agency for hiring consideration. If you are not hired for a position, your name usually remains on the eligible list for one to two years.

Most state government jobs are found in the state capital or large metropolitan areas. Expressing a willingness to relocate to other areas may improve your chances for obtaining a job.

Corrections Department Counselor and Administrator

Frank Spencer works closely with men between the ages of eighteen and sixty-four who are imprisoned in a state-operated facility for crimes ranging from petty theft to first-degree murder. Initially, Frank had to take a written exam to become a correctional counselor. Then as he advanced through the ranks to case manager, assistant group supervisor, and corrections supervisor to his present job as cell hall director, each promotion was based on either a written test or an experience and training rating.

Frank's initial qualifications for the position of correctional counselor were a bachelor's degree in psychology and experience working with juveniles. Since then, he has increased his knowledge of counseling by reading materials on psychology. Because his present position is more administrative, Frank does not do as much one-on-one or therapeutic group counseling as in his previous positions. In his work with individual inmates, he always tries to work with the inmate's family, since families can be an obstacle to an inmate's desire for a changed life after prison.

Working with counselors is voluntary for inmates; however, it is suggested that sex offenders, drug abusers, and those with character disorders participate in the counseling process in order to achieve better control over their lives. When Frank began as a corrections counselor, he imagined he would use his background in psychology to help hordes of inmates reap benefits. The reality was a much lower success rate. Now he appreciates seeing two out of twenty inmates make substantial improvement. What has been very gratifying about counseling inmates is that for every inmate Frank reaches, he also affects the inmate's family, so far more than one person develops new values.

Program Advisor for the Hearing Impaired

Pamela Bartels Gleason works with deaf and hard-of-hearing people, helping them function independently. She meets with them and their families to identify problems, offer suggestions, and refer them to the proper agencies for help. On a typical day on the job, you might find Pam convincing a large company that the deaf people working there need TDDs (Telecommunication Devices for the Deaf) and interpreters available for trainings, meetings, and performance reviews.

Pam also gives information on hearing impairment to people at schools, companies, and community service organizations so they will become more aware of how to interact with deaf and hard-of-hearing people. For example, Pam points out the importance of maintaining eye contact when talking with a deaf or hard-of-hearing person. Pam also trains people at businesses and agencies to use TDDs.

Part of the secret of Pam's success in helping the hearing impaired is that she has been deaf since she was thirteen months old. Not only can she communicate effectively with deaf persons in sign language, but she also serves as a role model, letting deaf people see how successfully she functions.

Originally, Pam believed that her career would be in medical laboratory technology. She graduated from junior college and worked in this area for one and a half years with the intention of obtaining a bachelor's degree in medical technology. Then one summer she worked at a leadership camp for the deaf and fell in love with working with people. She returned to college and changed her major to social work. After graduation, she worked with deaf and multiply handicapped children before taking her present position.

Pam's job satisfaction lies in having the opportunity and experience to work with deaf and hard-of-hearing people. Quoting the president of Gallaudet University (a college for the deaf), Pam tells the people with whom she works, "You can do anything except hear." And the hearing impaired believe her because they can see she is handling her job effectively.

Government Jobs at the County Level

County governments have an astounding variety of jobs to do. They act as agents of state governments in delivering a broad range of public services. It is within the areas of social, health, and corrections services that most Good Samaritans and humanitarians will find jobs, many as social workers.

Like state and federal government jobs, county positions are filled through an examination process. In addition to visiting the county personnel department and calling the local job information line, you can often find out about county jobs through advertisements in the media and notices on bulletin boards in social service organizations.

Social Workers

The vast majority of social workers in the United States are employed by government agencies. At the county level, social workers determine whether individuals or families are eligible for welfare funds and work with the elderly, the mentally ill, abused children, substance abusers, battered women, the homeless, pregnant women, the unemployed, and all the other people who are seriously in need in the county.

Social work is a profession. Even entry-level positions require job seekers to have a bachelor's degree in social work. In addition to course work for a bachelor's degree, an internship must be served. Furthermore, in more than half of the states, social workers must have a license or be registered in order to get a job. Many social workers who want greater job opportunities or supervisory positions also obtain master's degrees in social work. The average salary for social workers with master's degrees is more than $33,000 a year.

For more information about a career in social work, write to:

National Association of Social Workers
IC-Career Information
750 First Street NE, Suite 700
Washington, DC 20002
www.socialworkers.org

Social Worker in Child Protection. The highest-paid social workers are sometimes those who work in child protection because the job is so stressful. Imagine having to determine whether an abused child should remain in the home or be removed from the home environment. This is not an easy decision to make, even after very careful assessment of a situation, because there are so many unknowns. In addition, the decisions you make may be monitored by the press.

Mary Doyle is a county social worker in child protection in a large metropolitan area. Her usual caseload is from twelve to twenty families; fifteen is ideal. Unfortunately, child protection workers usually do not begin to work with a family until after the abuse or neglect has taken place and has been reported.

Mary tries to protect children from physical and sexual abuse and neglect. Families must work with her because it is a service mandated by the state when there have been reports of child abuse filed by nurses, doctors, teachers, relatives, neighbors, or others.

Mary does very little counseling. Instead, she meets with a family, carefully assesses the situation, and develops a case plan. She tries to get the family to agree on objectives and refers them to needed services, which often include counseling. Then she monitors the situation in order to continually assess how the family is doing. While the aim is to keep families together, at times Mary must have children removed from their homes in order to ensure their safety. This involves testifying in court.

Mary's professional background includes a master's degree in social work and experience in the Peace Corps and as a sales representative for an educational publisher. Reflecting on her career with child protection, Mary says, "This is a necessary job; someone must do it; you can't say that about all jobs." As a social worker, she sees people who have been victimized by the system. "It is hard," she says, "to be a stellar parent when you are impoverished." Mary believes that social workers have a mandate not just to help individuals but also to change society and institutions that may be oppressive.

Social Worker in Adoption Services. Some children become wards of the state because parental rights to the children have been terminated by the courts. These high-risk children—abused, abandoned, neglected, or handicapped—are the ones for whom Ed Holt tries to find families. His entire department celebrated when a worker in Ed's unit found a skilled family for an infant who was severely disabled and retarded because of a rare medical condition that required ongoing medical help.

Ed is unit supervisor of adoption services for a county and holds a master's degree in social work. Social workers in his unit have three specific duties. First, they become the child's guardian and make an assessment of the child's adoption needs. After the child is adopted, they make sure things are going well until the adoption is finalized. Second, these social workers make home studies to determine what a home is like, and they try to match parents and child. Third, they make a genetic search to determine a child's background so that the child and birth parents can locate each other, if they wish, after the child is nineteen years old.

For twelve years Ed worked in child protection, where positive feedback came from his coworkers rather than the families with whom he worked. Now, he is involved in major life events for children and their families. When all the pieces come together, and children and families find permanence that they might not have achieved without his help, Ed's career satisfaction is immense.

Government Jobs at the City Level

Cities typically are in charge of nuts-and-bolts governmental operations. They provide essential services such as police, fire, sanitation, water supply, street construction and maintenance, libraries, schools, and health protection. Still, there are jobs in most cities, especially large cities, for Good Samaritans and humanitarians. Information about employment can be obtained through personnel offices and, in larger cities, from a job information line.

City employees work under the civil service system and take exams for nearly all positions. What follows is a description of a few of the many jobs available in larger cities that allow Good Samaritans and humanitarians to help others.

- **Clinical social workers** provide direct social services in public health clinics. Duties include counseling selected families enrolled in health programs; assessing individual social problems and needs and interpreting them to other health-care team members; and making plans with families and patients for referrals to appropriate social agencies.
- **Crime prevention specialists** work with neighborhoods and communities to organize and implement community crime prevention plans. Specialists disseminate information, organize and maintain block clubs, and recruit, train, and develop neighborhood leaders.
- **Equal opportunity aides** make routine complaint and compliance review investigations, conduct interviews with potential complainants, prepare reports of investigations, and make recommendations.

- **Public health nurses** implement agency programs by promoting and maintaining the health of individuals, families, and the community. They teach, counsel, and provide appropriate preventative and rehabilitative measures in homes, day-care centers, and other community settings.
- **Chemical health specialists** work with students, staff, and parents in schools, developing strategies to prevent chemical abuse. They also counsel individuals.
- **Recreational leaders** plan, promote, and implement year-round recreation programs for neighborhoods, communities, and cities. They select, train, and recruit staff members.
- **Nutritionists** develop nutrition programs, counsel through home visits, and work at various clinics.
- **Registered professional nurses** provide nursing service to patients enrolled in various clinics and programs, counsel patients, develop care plans, and refer patients to appropriate agencies.
- **Resident planning aides** interview clients to determine eligibility for fuel and weatherization assistance, provide energy use and energy bill assistance, take applications for crisis funds, and counsel those facing disconnection of services.
- **Crime prevention youth coordinators** work on positive interaction between police and youth, coordinate youth crime prevention programs and programs to reduce victimization, and run youth training programs.

Jobs with the United Nations and Related Organizations

Idealistic Americans thinking of helping the extremely needy in developing countries often believe that the United Nations (UN) is the best source of jobs. This is not necessarily true. The United

Nations has very few job openings, and recruitment for these jobs is highly competitive. Many positions are only open to those holding doctorates who are also fluent in English and Spanish, French, or Arabic.

One reason for this shortage of jobs is a quota system, which divides the jobs in an organization, on a percentage system, based on the funds each country contributes. In addition, there is a desire to hire qualified people in developing countries to staff the programs within their own countries. For Americans who desire to work in developing countries, more job opportunities lie within private volunteer organizations, such as CARE and World Vision, than in the United Nations.

United Nations Children's Fund (UNICEF)

Working at UNICEF, an integral but semiautonomous part of the UN, is an opportunity for the Good Samaritan or humanitarian to promote peace and human welfare. UNICEF, the only United Nations organization dedicated exclusively to children, works for child protection, survival, and development within the framework of the Convention on the Rights of the Child, adopted unanimously for the United Nations General Assembly in 1989 and virtually universally ratified as of August 1997.

In cooperation with other United Nations agencies, governments, and nongovernmental organizations, UNICEF helps provide low-cost community-based services in primary health care, nutrition, basic education, and water and sanitation. It advocates for the rights of all children, especially girls. UNICEF also provides relief and rehabilitation assistance in emergency situations. Particular attention is focused on the major causes of death and disease among children under age five.

Today, nearly twelve million children die before the age of five, and estimates are that at least half of those deaths could be averted by a handful of low-cost health actions. For example, malnutrition deaths can be reduced by encouraging mothers to breast-feed and by having mothers weigh their children and monitor their growth. And many of the millions of children who die each year from measles, whooping cough, diphtheria, tetanus, polio, and tuberculosis could be saved by immunizations.

By using a community-based approach and a system of priority, low-cost, sustainable health measures, UNICEF has tackled the overwhelming problems facing children in developing countries. The work of UNICEF is carried out in more than 250 field offices, ranging in size from an outpost in an isolated area to a large office in a capital city, and serves 161 countries. Eighty-five percent of the more than seventy-three hundred UNICEF staff work in the field. Minimum requirements for the professional staff are a university degree and postgraduate study in a development-related discipline, such as development studies, economics, nutrition, primary education, public health, or social welfare. Professional work experience in a developing country is generally required, as is written and spoken fluency in English and French, Spanish, or Arabic.

Qualified people interested in working at UNICEF should write directly to:

Recruitment and Placement Service
Division of Human Resources
United Nations Children's Fund
UNICEF House
3 United Nations Plaza
New York, NY 10017
www.unicef.org

United Nations High Commissioner for Refugees (UNHCR)

"When you are kind to others, it not only changes you,
it changes the world."
—Harold Kushner

The protection of refugees and the seeking of lasting solutions to their problems are the two main functions of the United Nations High Commissioner for Refugees. These tasks are overwhelming because today there are roughly thirteen million refugees, mostly women and children, and the number continues to grow. Approximately one in every 115 people on the planet is exiled from his or her homeland each day. Through a variety of programs, UNHCR helps meet refugee needs for food, housing, medical care, education, and vocational training, as well as local integration, resettlement, or repatriation.

Good Samaritans and humanitarians can obtain more information by writing to:

United Nations High Commissioner for Refugees
PO Box 2500
CH-1211 Geneva 2
Switzerland
www.unhcr.ch

United Nations Development Program

In 1965, the United Nations combined its technical aid programs to form the United Nations Development Program (UNDP). This agency helps developing nations promote economic growth and better standards of living for their people through projects in agriculture, education, health, housing, industry, public administration, trade, and other related fields.

UNDP offers internship programs for graduate students and hires a small number of highly trained people for overseas assignments. Candidates should have a master's degree in an area such as business administration, economics, international relations, or public administration. They should also be able to speak at least two of the working UN languages and have two years of closely related experience.

For more information or a job application for overseas employment, write to:

UNDP Recruitment Section
Division of Personnel
One United Nations Plaza
New York, NY 10017
www.undp.org

You can learn more about other organizations within the
United Nations by reviewing the *Yearbook of the United Nations*,
available at the library.

CHAPTER FOUR

Providing Care and Compassion for the Sick and Suffering

istory is filled with people who have been Good Samaritans and humanitarians in the medical field. Some have devoted their entire lives to the medical issues of the neediest people. Their contributions to making the world a better place to live and providing comfort and much-needed medical care will continue to inspire others to follow in their footsteps.

Known throughout the world as "the saint of the gutters" for her unstinting help of the poor, the sick, and the dying, Mother Teresa was a symbol of the good that medical Good Samaritans and humanitarians can do. Her involvement with the people of India and the poor of the world began when she started a new religious order, the Missionaries of Charity, in 1946 after having studied nursing. Mother Teresa and members of her order first focused on helping the poor children in the streets. Then she and her fellow nuns gathered the dying from the streets and cared for them. In the mid-1950s, she worked with the Indian government to establish a leper colony. As the years passed, Mother Teresa's work expanded beyond India to treat lepers, the blind, the disabled, the aged, and the dying throughout the world. She also organized schools and orphanages. At the time of her death in 1997, her religious order had expanded to forty-five hundred nuns and religious brothers in almost six hundred homes for the poor in 126 countries.

For many people, Mother Teresa was the embodiment of hope and compassion. Her efforts were rewarded with many international prizes—the greatest being the Nobel Peace Prize in 1979. She accepted all of these awards on behalf of the poor and used any money accompanying them to fund her centers. The hallmark of her work was the respect that she gave to the individual with warm compassion and love. The work of Mother Teresa has been an inspiration to idealistic young people in the 1990s and beyond.

In the 1960s the work of Dr. Thomas Dooley in helping the people of Southeast Asia by establishing hospitals in remote areas was part of President Kennedy's inspiration to form the Peace Corps. Dr. Dooley described his philosophy of work and medical help on a person-to-person basis in these words:

> There is definitely a need in the world for American economic aid, but it so frequently does not reach down to the level of the villager. They know this airstrip or that water pump was made with American aid, but that is a cold unemotional thing. I believe medicine is one of the best weapons of foreign policy that we have. Here is one person talking to, working with, perhaps growing to love another person.

An earlier medical figure, Dr. Albert Schweitzer, also served humanity directly. At the age of thirty, he abandoned his careers as a noted writer and musician to study medicine with the goal of spending the rest of his life helping others. In 1913, he began practicing medicine in the African jungle, using a chicken coop as his first consulting room. Over the years, he built a large hospital where thousands of Africans were treated each year. When he was awarded the Nobel Peace Prize in 1952, he used the prize money to expand the hospital and establish a leper colony.

Being a Good Samaritan or humanitarian in the area of health care is decidedly not the sole province of twentieth-century medical figures. Today, Florence Nightingale is considered the founder of the modern nursing profession. But British soldiers knew her as the "Lady with the Lamp" when she walked through the hospital's halls late at night, caring for those wounded in the Crimean War. Five hundred wounded soldiers were hospitalized in Turkey without cots or medical supplies when Florence arrived. She had those who were well enough clean the makeshift hospital and demanded supplies from the British government. Once the hospital was running better, she even taught the convalescing soldiers to read and write. Because of her work during the Crimean War, the United States asked Florence for her help in setting up hospitals during the Civil War.

Clara Barton was another well-known humanitarian nurse. Early in her career, she carried supplies to soldiers and nursed those wounded on Civil War battlefields. She became known as the "Angel of the Battlefield." She later went on to help found the American Red Cross. In between, she ran a missing-soldiers operation that was part of the effort to heal the nation.

Today's medicine is high technology, but this doesn't mean that there aren't many Good Samaritans and humanitarians all over the world using their skills on a one-to-one basis to help people who have special needs. Many health-care professionals devote a few hours a week or one day a month to clinics for the needy. It is also increasingly common for health-care professionals to volunteer their service for a week or longer, in the United States or abroad, caring for needy people who have no other access to medical help. There are still others willing to devote months, years, or a lifetime to working in areas where limited medical help is available or with people who cannot readily afford medical care.

Preparing for a Career in Medicine

In order to serve humanity as a doctor or nurse, professional training and licensing are essential. The path to becoming a doctor is a long one—usually eleven years, including four years of college, four years of medical school, and three years in residency. Then it is necessary to pass a licensing examination. For those who train as specialists, up to seven more years may be spent in residency training. If you want to become a doctor, you must have the desire to serve patients, be self-motivated, and be able to survive the pressures and long hours of medical education and practice.

Nurses do not need nearly as many years of training as doctors do. Most licensed practical nurses who work under the direction of doctors and registered nurses have completed a nursing program that lasts about a year and have passed a licensing examination. Registered nurses complete programs lasting from two to five years, depending on the educational degree program in which they participate.

Doctors are among the highest earners of any occupation, averaging more than $100,000 a year after expenses. Full-time salaried registered nurses average close to $700 in weekly earnings, while licensed practical nurses average approximately $450 per week. However, both doctors and nurses who elect to work for humanitarian organizations both in the United States and abroad will earn considerably less, possibly only living expenses.

Health-Care Programs in the United States

Medical care is expensive in the United States. Not being able to afford health care when it is needed can be disastrous. Federal, state, and local government units and many private nonprofit organizations have set up programs to provide free or low-cost health care. Within this vast array of programs, health professionals who are Good Samaritans and humanitarians can easily find careers ministering to the needy. Their work environment may not be the antiseptic quarters of a modern hospital but rather a rural or inner-city clinic, a shelter for the homeless, a mobile van, or even the streets.

A Federal Health-Care Program for the Homeless

More than 130 federally funded health-care programs for the homeless treated a total of approximately 750,000 patients in 1997. Dr. Peter Kim has worked in one of these programs, the Homeless Initiative, in a metropolitan area for four years. Many federally funded programs have a sliding fee scale, and people pay what they can afford, according to certain poverty guidelines. However, in this program, treatment is free.

Dr. Kim works full-time with a medical assistant traveling between shelters and homeless service providers. Their patients know the travel schedule. On a typical day, Dr. Kim and his assistant might be at a family shelter in the morning and at a day center for the homeless in the afternoon.

Dr. Kim is not like the doctors most people are accustomed to seeing in an office. He must carry all the equipment and supplies he needs with him. When he treats a patient, he must be able to provide the necessary medication or medical aids right on the spot. Going to where the patient is staying creates a trust and bond. Individuals who have usually been resistant to visiting the hospital or the doctor will seek medical care.

The Lamb's Center

Founded by the Lamb's Manhattan Church of the Nazarene, the Lamb's Center began providing primary health care, health education, and social services to the homeless and the needy of the Times Square area in New York City in 1982. Dr. Mark Dollar worked as medical director of the clinic along with registered nurse Karen Storz and a volunteer staff of other health-care professionals.

The doctor explains that treating the homeless is almost a medical specialty because homelessness brings special medical problems. "You have to put disease in the context of homelessness," he says. "You don't send a homeless diabetic out of the hospital on insulin. He can't refrigerate it. He'll get mugged for the needles, and on insulin, if he can't get food, his blood sugar will drop too low." For this reason, Dr. Dollar treated homeless diabetic patients with oral medication, even though it is usually less effective than insulin. The doctor goes on to point out the difficulty of treating a homeless person. "If a person lives in a house, you give him a prescription for antibiotics and tell him to stay off his feet and change the dressing twice a day. That's really impossible for the homeless. So they end up in the hospital very sick a week later when the infection has spread. Most emergency room doctors do not see homelessness as a medical problem in itself that should affect treatment, but it has to be," adds Dr. Dollar.

At the Lamb's Center, Dr. Dollar saw about twenty-five men, women, and children a day. In his role as a doctor to the homeless, he was part of a new breed of medical professionals dealing with the neediest members of American society. Today, the center no longer offers medical services, and Dr. Dollar is now trained as a psychiatrist. He continues his humanitarian efforts by working in a public hospital treating the indigent and also has a small private practice.

Gennesaret Free Clinic

Today over 350 volunteers are carrying on Dr. James Trippi's vision to provide outreach health-care services for the homeless. The organization got its name from the biblical site of Gennesaret, where people brought the sick to touch the fringe of Jesus's cloak in hopes of being healed.

Desiring to serve others, the cardiovascular specialist first thought of missionary service. However, he didn't wish to uproot his family and decided that urgent help was just as needed within his own community. Working with volunteer doctors and nurses, donated equipment, and free samples of medicine, Dr. Trippi's group started a weekly free health clinic at a homeless shelter. Today the group has a mobile medical van serving four sites and clinics in seven shelters five days a week. Gennesaret Clinic also provides transitional housing for eight homeless men after hospitalization to encourage full recuperation. The volunteers are physicians, nurses, nurse practitioners, physician and medical assistants, medical students, dentists, and other concerned individuals. A paid staff of nine handles fund-raising, medical records, and coordinating the volunteers, including a social worker who deals with the issues of homeless women and men.

Dr. Trippi feels that the Gennesaret Clinic volunteers are not only healing the homeless people but also having a very healing experience themselves. Furthermore, he has seen how dedicated Good Samaritans and humanitarians can make a difference, even with such an overwhelming problem as caring for the medical needs of the homeless.

Dr. Trippi believes that his organization proves that volunteering can be easily integrated into the lives of busy health-care professionals. Since volunteers sometimes suffer from burnout, medical volunteers at his clinic are usually limited to one two- or three-hour shift every four to six weeks. In this way, volunteers are always looking forward to their next shift.

Doctor of AIDS Patients

Dr. Judith A. Deutsch was a Fellow in Infectious Disease when the AIDS epidemic started. She began taking care of AIDS patients in the mid-1980s and was immediately struck by the tragedy this disease brought to their lives. Not only did AIDS patients have a severe, disabling, and fatal illness, but they were also frequently social outcasts—rejected by their families, friends, communities, and even doctors.

In 1987, Dr. Deutsch was recruited from the faculty of the University of Louisville to work for Indiana University's Department of Medicine. One of the myriad responsibilities of her position is providing primary care services for between twenty and thirty patients with AIDS.

Dr. Deutsch's interest in helping AIDS patients extends beyond her career commitments. She volunteers as the medical director of the Damien Center, a nonprofit organization helping AIDS patients, and she serves as chairperson for the steering committee for the HIV Services Planning Program for Indiana.

Dr. Deutsch believes that AIDS has made people aware of the inequities in the American health-care system. Looking to the future, this Good Samaritan would like to be a part of improving the health-care delivery system for the poor, stigmatized, and medically needy. She wants to continue her efforts to educate health-care providers in giving humane and competent care. Dr. Deutsch gains career satisfaction from making the world a better place for at least a small group of people. She is particularly satisfied when she can facilitate humane decisions about the care of people with AIDS.

Health-Care Programs Abroad

The victims of poverty, war, and oppression in developing countries—especially the children—desperately need medical help. It is estimated that as many as 7 percent of these children are critically ill and dying daily from lack of proper nourishment and health care. Developing countries often do not have the means or skilled medical help their citizens need. Opportunities abound for Good Samaritans and humanitarians possessing medical skills to respond to this desperate need for medical assistance.

The medical facilities in many developing countries are primitive; supplies are limited, and modern medical equipment is often nonexistent. But here the chance to make a real difference in people's lives exists for every trained health-care provider—not only in directly treating people but also in providing health education.

Traditionally, much of the medical aid provided to developing countries was delivered through church organizations and their medical missionaries. This support continues today. You can find out more about medical career and volunteer opportunities connected to church groups by contacting any of the organizations listed in Appendix B. In addition, you can investigate opportunities with nonprofit American organizations engaged in international humanitarian efforts by contacting any of the InterAction member organizations listed in Appendix A.

Kissy United Methodist Church Eye Hospital

Dr. Lowell A. Gess, an ophthalmologist, had seminary training but also felt called to practice medicine as a way to share the gospel. Since his graduation from medical school, he and his wife, a nurse, have repeatedly gone to Africa as volunteer medical missionaries, often for years at a time. During his time in the United States, Dr. Gess has been actively involved in the latest of advances in ophthalmology and has published several professional papers.

In 1975, after several three-year stints in Africa, mainly in Sierra Leone, Dr. Gess opened a private practice in Minnesota. However, he continued to spend three months each year in Sierra Leone. In 1983, the Kissy United Methodist Church Eye Hospital was built in Freetown to serve the four million Sierra Leoneans and fifteen million other people in surrounding countries. A group of forty volunteer ophthalmologists have each worked from one to three months over the years until recently, when civil war and political instability have prevented them from going to Sierra Leone. These doctors underwrote their own expenses and brought along medicines and supplies.

Since 1990, Dr. Gess and his wife have responded to invitations to do surgery and teaching programs in countries such as Kenya, Ghana, Zambia, Zimbabwe, Mozambique, Haiti, Bolivia, Vietnam, China, and Mongolia. Their oldest son, Timothy, is an ophthalmologist also participating in volunteer surgery trips. When Dr. Gess started working three-year stints as a career missionary, his salary was only $2,800 a year. Today, medical missionaries for his church earn a base salary of approximately $17,000 to $18,000 plus the rental of a home.

In the future, Dr. Gess looks forward to a network of eye-care sites being established in African countries. While the ideal is to have the centers staffed by ophthalmologists living in Africa, there aren't enough trained specialists available yet. However, much is being accomplished through the efforts of volunteer ophthalmologists like Dr. Gess.

This Good Samaritan's career has brought him many moments of satisfaction. Imagine being present when blind patients experience sight. They can hardly contain their joy—a joy that is vicariously enjoyed by each member of the staff. There is similar reward when patients are fitted with eyeglasses that enable them to read and to see the world around them. There is also the fulfillment of treating and preventing glaucoma and other sight-endangering diseases. And as Christian missionaries, the doctors are always especially thrilled when, because of the eye ministry, they can reach their patients in a spiritual way.

The opportunities for career satisfaction and jobs in missions like Dr. Gess's are limitless. The help that Dr. Gess and the eye clinic staff give to others is making a genuine difference in the eye problems suffered by Africans.

A Nazarene Mission Hospital

Dr. Lemoyne Pringle and Dr. Michael Pyle are physicians who were also missionaries. Together, they worked out an unusual arrangement that tied their two families closely together. The families shared careers, homes, cars, and even pets. Instead of doing a four-year missionary tour, each doctor did a two-year rotation. That way, both doctors were able to keep their medical skills current and still be financially self-supporting.

The call to missionary service came to each doctor separately. For Dr. Pyle, the call came during his junior year in medical school, when he and another physician were seeing a hundred sick, dirty, and destitute Haitians every day during a month's mission in Haiti. Dr. Pringle grew up attending a Nazarene church that placed a heavy emphasis on mission work. As a youth, he often helped roll bandages to send overseas, and missionaries home on furlough often stayed with his family. He made the decision as a teenager to become a doctor because it would allow him to combine his aptitude for science with missionary work.

In Swaziland, Africa, the two doctors worked in a Nazarene-run mission hospital in the town of Manzini. The people were poor, and the need was great. When Dr. Pyle first went overseas, there were only seven surgeons for the entire country of eight hundred thousand, which caused an extraordinarily stressful work situation for him. Fortunately, the situation improved.

Both doctors made a financial sacrifice, since their stint in Africa paid only $9,000 a year. But both doctors thought more about the rewards they received rather than the sacrifices they made. As Dr. Pyle says, "If I left my practice in the United States, they'd find a surgeon to replace me, but in Swaziland, I really made a difference. Things would be worse without me."

The two doctors felt that by sharing missionary duties they would not lose touch with people back at their own church. While one doctor was in Africa, the other could keep in touch with him and bring his needs before the church. Also, their continuing presence in a small Midwestern community served as a catalyst for a growing interest in the needs of the Swazi people.

Of course, there were disadvantages to the two-year arrangement. Neither doctor had enough time to become fully immersed in the African culture or to become a fluent speaker of Siswati, the native language. Both families adapted well to life on both sides of the ocean, but there were obvious sacrifices. The children made new friends and then had to say good-bye to them.

The two families overlapped for a two-month period in the United States. It was a time for them to compare notes before separating again. "Because we both trust in God, we were able to trust in one another," says Dr. Pyle. "We made a decision to do it, and the friendship followed." Today, the two doctors are back in the United States where both are active in their churches.

Project HOPE (Health Opportunity for People Everywhere)

Project HOPE is a nonprofit organization that trains and educates local health-care workers to assume responsibility for their countries' own health delivery systems. More than a million health professionals have been trained by the organization in more than seventy countries. Project HOPE was founded in 1958 by Dr. William B. Walsh, a heart specialist. Since then, thousands of doctors, nurses, and other health professionals have helped to develop a core of local experts who become self-sustaining by the end of Project HOPE's stay in a region.

Dr. Walsh began Project HOPE with a former U.S. Navy ship that was refitted to become the world's first peacetime hospital ship. Between its first voyage in 1960 and its last voyage in 1974, the SS *Hope* visited twelve countries with its cargo of health-care professionals and medical technology. To implement long-term education programs, medical teams often remained behind after the ship sailed on. Because of the demand for help from land-locked countries, the ship was retired in 1974, and Project HOPE became a land-based organization.

Project HOPE's programs include training medical personnel in specialties ranging from cardiovascular medicine, nursing, and community health improvement to surgery, preventive dentistry, health-care administration, and medical textbook distribution. The organization also works with governments to develop health-care systems and facilities and provides humanitarian assistance during periods of war, national crisis, and natural disaster. The success of Project HOPE can be measured by the people it has affected directly—the Chinese children whose life-threatening heart defects have been corrected by Project HOPE surgeons, the women in Central America who have learned how best to care for their infants, and the people of war-torn Bosnia who have received needed medicines.

Project HOPE has made an impact on the health programs of many nations. In Egypt, nursing education programs have been strengthened and expanded so that the country will come closer to the international standard of four nurses per doctor. In Chile, surgeons, cardiologists, anesthesiologists, and nurses, as well as surgical assistants and other technicians, have been trained in their respective roles in preoperative cardiac assessment and post-operative care of patients in intensive care. In the remote areas of Haiti, education programs have reduced malnutrition, diarrheal disease, and communicable diseases.

Qualifications. Project HOPE is looking for doctors, nurses, dentists, biomedical engineers, health-care administrators, health economists, physical therapists, midwives, and others with medical skills. Medical personnel working in the field may volunteer their time or be paid living expenses; however, many are salaried. Typically, people work for a year; some work as long as ten years. Shorter stints of just a week or more are also possible.

Many people have worked on different Project HOPE programs at various times in their lives. Some of the people on the first voyage of the SS *Hope* are still working on programs. If you are interested in learning more about Project HOPE, contact:

Project HOPE
255 Carter Hall Lane
Millwood, VA 22646
www.projhope.org

A Project HOPE Doctor. What makes an American pediatrician want to work in the third world? For Dr. James Belt, it's the time he spent working with and helping the people on the impoverished West Indian island of Grenada for Project HOPE. His first experience on Grenada was a two-month stint after the American intervention left the island without anyone to provide medical care. At that time, the United States government asked Project HOPE to oversee the delivery of health care on Grenada.

Dr. Belt returned to Grenada for a year in 1987 to recruit and hire doctors so that pediatrics and surgery could be transferred from Project HOPE to the Grenadian government. "The secret of recruiting," according to Dr. Belt, "is finding people who can work well with what is available." In the United States, for example, there is a wide choice of antibiotics, but in Grenada only four antibiotics are usually accessible. "Down here," he says about Grenada, "you've got to be happy with what you've got. Once you begin to fight the system, the system will eat you up."

A typical workday would begin around 8:00 A.M. with meetings with other Project HOPE doctors to discuss problems and do paperwork. Then the doctors would go to an outlying clinic— often an hour away—by van. "In Grenada," Dr. Belt says, "when you get to the clinic you start, and when you finish, you finish." Despite the lack of equipment, facilities, and the latest medical technology, Dr. Belt believes that much can be accomplished in the clinics.

After his assignment in Grenada, Dr. Belt went to China for one year as the program director for Project HOPE. He was responsible for the management and development of collaborative programs with five Chinese universities. In one program, at Xian Medical University, high school students were trained for three years in rudimentary medical procedures such as taking blood pressures and temperatures and giving first aid. Since many Chinese live in rural areas, these so-called "barefoot doctors" can do a lot to treat minor ailments. In the future, Dr. Belt plans to be involved in short-term assignments with Project HOPE and has already spent time providing humanitarian aid in former Russian republics.

Westlane Christian Church Volunteers

The Westlane Christian Church, a church in a Midwest city, sends all types of workers into Haiti, one of the most underdeveloped and densely populated countries in the western hemisphere. "Going to Haiti is almost like going back in time ten thousand years," according to Dr. Bob Nelson, a volunteer who worked for a week in Ticousin, a small village. The village, which isn't even on Haiti's official map, doesn't have electricity, telephones, or running water. Dr. Nelson went to Ticousin as part of a team of fourteen workers sponsored by the Westlane Christian Church. The team consisted of medical workers, carpenters, and plumbers.

Before they arrived, villagers, under the direction of local missionaries, had erected a temporary medical clinic using bamboo poles and palm leaves. The examining tables were similar to park picnic tables. Dr. Nelson, a cancer specialist, worked as a general practitioner. The other medical members of the team were nurses and a nurse practitioner. The missionaries announced that there would be a clinic only one day before it was scheduled to open. So eager were the residents for medical help that seven hundred people came to the clinic on the day it opened. If the announcement had been made a week earlier, it is likely that at least two thousand people would have sought help.

The biggest medical problems in Ticousin are infectious diseases, skin diseases, dysentery, malaria, malnutrition, parasites, and tuberculosis. Because no other medical team was scheduled to come to Ticousin for three months, Dr. Nelson and the other members of his medical group treated only the people that they believed could be adequately treated. Fortunately, 90 percent of the people who came to the clinic fell into this category. The medical group also identified people with major problems and referred those people to other doctors.

The medical group at the clinic spent only six and a half hours a day seeing patients. The examining hours were short because so much time had to be spent mixing salves and packaging pills. In addition, transportation time was long because the medical team stayed seventeen miles from the clinic, which was only accessible by a dirt road.

Dr. Nelson and the other Good Samaritans on the medical team experienced immense satisfaction from helping people who did not have regular medical care. During their brief stay, the lives of two very sick babies were saved and hundreds of other people were significantly helped. The medical needs of the Haitians made such an impact on Dr. Nelson that he planned to return to Haiti in 1991. In preparation for this trip, he wrote to drug companies, asking for supplies. Unfortunately, he could not make the trip because of political conditions, but the drugs were sent to Haiti. Good Samaritans and humanitarians with medical training will find that opportunities to help in third world countries exist in programs within many of their churches.

Other Medical Programs

World Vision is the world's largest Christian international relief and development agency. The organization has a variety of health projects in Asia, Africa, and Latin America. Currently, medical health specialists with strong backgrounds in public health can find career, short-term, and volunteer jobs focused on child survival, HIV/AIDS prevention, nutrition promotion, and health reform projects. You can find out more about World Vision at www.worldvision.org and in Chapter 5.

The International Rescue Committee (IRC) was founded in 1933 at the request of Albert Einstein to help people trapped in Hitler's Germany and escaping to free countries. Since then, IRC has become the leading private American agency devoted to the cause of refugees. With the help of doctors, nurses, and public health workers, IRC provides medical aid to enable sick, hungry, and wounded refugees to survive. This is a gigantic task that should appeal to Good Samaritans and humanitarians with the needed medical training. You can learn more about the IRC and job opportunities online at www.intrescom.org.

Local Health-Care Programs

Within every community, there are people who truly need the help of Good Samaritans and humanitarians with medical skills. Two groups especially needing this help are the elderly living in nursing homes and people with terminal illnesses who are facing death. Not only do career opportunities exist focused on helping these groups, but volunteers are also needed.

Valley Convalescent Hospital

The Valley Convalescent Hospital is a fifty-nine-bed nursing home in Watsonville, California. The average age of the patients is the mideighties. Mary Foust, the former head nurse, began working at the convalescent hospital in 1972. Most of the other nurses have been there ten to fifteen years.

Mary's nursing job was not a typical one. She did routine, everyday tasks, which included checking the ill, handling paperwork, feeding patients, checking the correctness of diet, and helping distribute meal trays. But there was much more to her job than this. Like anyone else, the elderly need conversation, hugs, and kisses, and Mary helped to provide them.

All of the nurses at this nursing home share Mary's compassion for the elderly. They become quite attached to their patients, and they find it very upsetting when one suddenly dies. Without the loving care of these nurses, life would be very lonely for the nursing home residents, some of whom enjoy only infrequent visits from family and friends.

North Hospice

North Hospice in Minneapolis offers hospital and home-based programs for the terminally ill and their families. The modern hospice movement began in the late 1960s when a new conception of medical care, palliative care, emerged. Palliative care focuses not on looking for cures but on the comfort needs of the dying. While palliative care primarily addresses the physical needs of patients, their psychological, emotional, and spiritual needs are of equal importance. The task of the team of nurses, physicians, social workers, family support personnel, and volunteers is to guide the dying patients and their families through this difficult journey.

The staff at North Hospice is generally age thirty or older. Most staff members have worked in other medical facilities before coming to the hospice. Choosing to work at the hospice is often connected to a personal experience, especially the death of a loved one. Being a hospice worker can be a difficult job because it forces people to look at their own mortality. However, the dedicated Good Samaritans and humanitarians working for hospices know that they have valuable aid to give to the dying and their families.

Most hospice care in the United States is given in homes. Only in crisis situations are the patients hospitalized. The majority of hospice patients are cancer victims, but there are also people suffering from a variety of illnesses, including terminal heart disease, chronic lung problems, and Lou Gehrig's disease.

Hospice patients are generally seen in their homes once or twice a week but may be visited as frequently as every day, if needed. The social workers and family support personnel work with both patients and their families. These hospice workers may visit patients as a team or individually. Their goal is to help patients remain at home and be comfortable for as long as possible.

Hospice work does not end with the death of the patient but continues through the grieving period, providing support for the survivors. Volunteers and staff maintain contact with families after the death and are available for counseling, support, and sometimes just a hug.

Other Needy Populations

Others who especially need the care of Good Samaritans with medical expertise are sufferers of Alzheimer's disease, substance abusers, burn victims, the mentally retarded and mentally ill, victims of AIDS, and people with serious long-term illnesses such as muscular dystrophy, multiple sclerosis, and cystic fibrosis. Good Samaritans can find jobs ministering to these special-needs people in hospitals and clinics and through home nursing programs.

CHAPTER FIVE

Serving Others and Your Faith Through Religious Careers

"What we have done for ourselves alone dies with us. What we have done for others and the world remains and is immortal."
—Albert Pine

There are many religious faiths and groups throughout the world. Even though these religions have diverse beliefs, you will often find they have a common mission of helping others who are less fortunate. All religions need good laborers—people who desire to help all of God's people, from the starving children in Africa to the aged in nursing homes. A wide variety of jobs within religious organizations are perfect for the Good Samaritan or humanitarian. These laborers may be rabbis consoling the dying in hospitals, chaplains counseling substance abusers, nuns working with prison inmates, or missionaries teaching students in third world countries.

Just like other Good Samaritans and humanitarians, those choosing careers within religious organizations are seeking to make a difference in people's lives. They also share a deep, personal faith, which is the reason they have chosen a career within a religious group.

Is a Religious Career Right for You?

People who choose a religious career find that as they serve, their faith grows through involvement in their ministry, and their work fulfills their need to serve humanity. Are you destined to find satisfaction in some type of religious career? Perhaps you are, if you answer yes to the following questions:

1. Are you a person of deep faith?
2. Do you want to share God with others?
3. Do you want a career that will offer you more than fulfilling your own personal needs?

All religions are looking for men and women who have a vision of what the world could be. Religious careers call for people to have certain characteristics. How many of the following characteristics can you say you have?

1. I am able to turn compassion into cheerful deeds.
2. I am able to clearly explain the Bible to others.
3. I can organize people, ideas, and tasks for God's service.
4. I am sensitive to people who are suffering, troubled, and discouraged.
5. I easily know when others need help.
6. I enjoy explaining the principles of the Bible to others.
7. I enjoy leading others to God.
8. I enjoy caring for others for God's sake.
9. I can communicate with people about their spiritual needs.
10. I give freely of my finances to help do God's work.
11. I could lower my standard of living for God and God's people.
12. I can share God's love with people who are hurting.
13. I like to do work that helps others.
14. I have the ability to delegate important tasks.
15. I can discriminate between good and evil in the world.

16. I can identify with people who are hurting, and I want to help them.
17. I feel fulfilled by God's word.
18. I enjoy using my creative ability in art and music to serve God.

People considering a religious career will be able to find a specific area that suits their talent, whether it is leadership, teaching, evangelism, art, music, or missionary work.

Education and Training
In some churches, you can be a member of the clergy without a college degree or seminary training. However, most denominations expect their ministers to have completed college and graduated from a theological school. The undergraduate degree does not necessarily have to be in theology. The typical four-year program of theological studies includes courses such as scripture, fundamentals in pastoral theology, church history, comparative religion, and liturgical theology. Special programs are available to candidates entering the religious life at a later age.

Earnings and Hours
A love of God and a strong desire to help others draw far more people into religious careers than the hope of ever making a lot of money. The earnings of ministers and other religious workers vary widely. Be assured that churches do not let their ministers or the ministers' families starve.

Salaries are based on one's age, years of experience, education, and denomination. The number of people in a congregation, their incomes, and the location of the church will also have an effect on salaries and benefits.

Many ministers receive benefits such as free housing, utility payments, meals, hospitalization, transportation, pensions, and paid vacations. Including benefits, Protestant ministers earn approximately $40,000 a year, while the earnings of rabbis range from $38,000 to $62,000. While Roman Catholic priests may have salaries under $10,000, with the addition of benefits, their earnings average almost $30,000 a year.

Almost all religious workers work long, irregular hours. Many ministers are really on call twenty-four hours a day. Deaths, accidents, illnesses, and family crises do not occur according to any schedule. Furthermore, ministers' evenings and weekends are often devoted to church services, meetings, and counseling.

A Calling to Serve

For many people, choosing a religious career is easy because they believe that they have been called to this career by God. Not everyone who decides on a religious career, however, gets a divine calling. Some people, like Tom Clegg, a Catholic priest, wrestle with the idea of a calling to serve God for years. After high school, Tom went into the seminary, but he dropped out after six months and tried the insurance business. The second time he entered the seminary, he stayed a year and a half before leaving to get a degree in education.

During his senior year in college, Tom decided to follow in his father's footsteps, and he became a firefighter for twenty months. The sudden death of a young man Tom had coached in Little League made him decide to try the seminary again. He remained undecided about becoming a priest until a few months before his ordination, when an older priest put his mind to rest by saying that you can never be 100 percent sure about anything in this life.

Fifteen years later, Tom has no regrets about his choice to become a priest. His career path has allowed him to help many people from all walks of life. He started as an associate pastor at Christ the King parish in Indianapolis. Tom was under the supervision of the pastor, and his job responsibilities included early morning masses, hospital visits, and leading small groups of people who wished to join the church. He also helped the pastor with the baptisms, weddings, and funerals of parishioners.

After two years, Tom became a pastor at St. Catherine's and St. James's churches in Indianapolis. Within twelve months, the parishes decided to consolidate so Father Tom could better serve the needs of the families. The parishioners submitted three names to the bishop for the new parish. "Good Shepherd" was chosen, and a new parish was born. Within two years, they raised the money to build a new church. Father Tom pastored the Good Shepherd church for ten and one-half years.

Father Tom's next challenge took him to Sacred Heart Parish in Jeffersonville, Indiana, where he serves approximately six hundred families and celebrates about twenty-five baptisms, twenty-five weddings, and twenty-five funerals each year. He also helps to run the parish school. In the very near future, Father Tom will likely become the pastor of a second nearby parish in Jeffersonville. This opportunity will double his responsibilities.

Father Tom finds great fulfillment from helping the families in his parish. He feels it is a gift to be invited in during the critical times of people's lives and to help them celebrate during their joyous times. This keeps him motivated because rather than simply enduring his vocation, he feels alive in the priesthood.

Tikkun Olam—Repairing the World

From a young age, Dr. John Abrams's family taught him the importance of leaving the world a better place than when he entered it. Growing up in the Jewish community, he was taught to improve the community in which he lives through the philosophy *Tikkun Olam*, meaning "repairing the world." *Tikkun Olam* encompasses the inner and outer life through service to society by helping those in need and through service to the divine. This is something that Dr. Abrams has practiced throughout his life, and his children now follow in his footsteps.

Despite leading a busy life as an eye physician and surgeon, Dr. Abrams has lived this philosophy through his involvement in several foundations. In 2001, Dr. Abrams joined the Indiana Pacers Foundation board of directors, which funds youth sports and education programs. He is motivated by this foundation's focus on strengthening youth and increasing opportunities for youth with new partnerships. As vice president of the board for the Jewish Federation of Greater Indianapolis, Dr. Abrams has reached the elderly, the mentally handicapped, nursing homes, Hebrew school, and organizations overseas. The Jewish Federation of Greater Indianapolis offers the opportunity to maintain and strengthen the Jewish community and their efforts to keep a philanthropic presence in the Indianapolis community.

Dr. John Abrams's presence in the medical and Jewish communities has allowed this humanitarian to make a difference in many ways. A graduate of Indiana University, Dr. Abrams has established multiple scholarships that assist students to attend the Indiana University Medical School. His establishment of the Linda Craig Memorial Scholarship through the Pacer Foundation enables an undergraduate student to pursue a career in medicine, sports medicine, or physical therapy.

Dr. Abrams has received numerous awards and recognition, but he is not seeking recognition; he simply wants to make a difference in his community and follow the beliefs of his faith to repair the world and make it a better place.

Leading a Congregation

Since the days of the Old Testament, whenever people were in trouble, homeless, or depressed, they turned to their church leaders to seek advice. These leaders were considered the authorities in the community. Today, ministers, pastors, and rabbis still garner this respect.

Modern-day religious leaders, like those of the past, do not have the luxury of devoting their time solely to their congregations. They are also responsible for maintaining the physical plant, keeping financial records, supervising staff members, and participating in community affairs.

Rabbi of a Congregation in a Large City

Rabbi Jonathan Stein of the Reform branch of Judaism was attracted to the rabbinate because it allowed him to use his skills and talents in a Jewish setting, which has always been important to him. The job of a rabbi can be very demanding; in the spring and fall, it is not unusual for Rabbi Stein to work a seventy-hour week and still not get everything done.

A typical day for Rabbi Stein may include speaking to a group of three hundred people, counseling a dying man in the hospital, teaching Hebrew to a class of four-year-olds, talking to an excited couple about their approaching marriage, or counseling and referring members of the congregation to specialists for help. The word *rabbi* means teacher, and the rabbi's function is to educate his congregation. Rabbi Stein does this in his services as he explains Jewish values, history, ideas, and perspective to his congregation.

Rabbi Stein believes that all clergy, regardless of their denomination, have many things in common. All have one-on-one relationships with people as a major part of their ministry, and all share important moments and rites of passage with their congregations.

Small-Town Parish Priest

With only one part-time assistant, Father Francis J. Eckstein ministers to twenty-two hundred people. He takes care of all their spiritual needs, from baptizing to burying the dead. He sees himself as a mediator between God and the people of his congregation. Although he feels that his primary task is to lead his congregation along the spiritual path, he also spends considerable time at administrative tasks, such as overseeing an operating budget of more than $600,000.

Pastor in a Suburban Community

The major focus of Pastor Tom Paino's ministry is pastoral care, from handling crises to visiting shut-ins. A significant block of his time, however, is spent preparing for services. He also is busy administering a staff of five full-time ministers, four counselors, and four secretaries. He describes his work as a "crazy" job that is only possible for those who feel that they were called to help others. He regularly works an eighty-hour week in order to spend more time with members of his congregation.

Chaplains—Serving the Spiritual Needs of a Group

Chaplains are members of the clergy who minister in a specific setting, such as a hospital, prison, police or fire department, college campus, military base or combat zone, or even in a particular industry. They may be employed by the group to whom they minister or by a church or other institution. Their duties involve counseling, leading worship services, and working with families. They are constantly ministering to different people, often in crisis situations. Their work is a personal ministry in helping others.

Most people who become chaplains already have bachelor's degrees in spirituality, education, philosophy, or pastoral ministry, along with master's degrees. An additional year or more of special in-depth training is required for these people to become chaplains. Certification is also required to secure a chaplain's position in many institutions.

Hospital Chaplain

Most chaplains work in a hospital environment. The chaplain can be part of the hospital's paid personnel or may be sent by a nearby council or other community agency. As part of the hospital staff, a chaplain is treated like any other employee and receives all the same benefits. Hospital chaplain salaries start at around $25,000 per year and can go as high as $40,000.

Hospitals have chaplains on duty or at least on call twenty-four hours a day. The larger a hospital is, the greater the number of chaplains of different faiths. With the increasing popularity of holistic medicine, the chaplain now often helps with healing the patient's spirit and mind alongside medical colleagues who are working to heal the body.

Sister Rita Ann Wade of the Sisters of Providence is a hospital chaplain at a suburban hospital. She does not wear a habit, and she finds it easy to work with people of all faiths. With a degree in education and teaching experience behind her, Sister Rita Ann returned to school to obtain training in clinical pastoral education. After receiving this education, she obtained her present position as a hospital chaplain.

Sister Rita Ann finds career satisfaction in being able to intervene for families in situations where they need help. For example, chaplains can get information about how a patient is doing in surgery to help relieve some of the family's anxiety. Being a hospital chaplain is often a crisis ministry, often involving death, dying, and trauma. Chaplains like Sister Rita Ann try to bring faith, scriptural hope, and comfort to patients and their families as well as the hospital staff.

Correctional Institution Chaplain

From minimum- to maximum-security prisons, chaplains minister to hundreds of thousands of incarcerated people. Almost every state or federal prison and delinquent youth center has either a full-time or a part-time chaplain.

Like hospital chaplains, who help people deal with feelings of grief, anxiety, and hopelessness, prison chaplains also help people deal with anger, brutality, and despair. They help prisoners with substance-abuse problems and relationship problems. And, of course, prison chaplains try to open spiritual doors to closed minds and nurture and challenge existing faith.

Doris Woodruff serves as chaplain at a women's prison. With an undergraduate degree in journalism and art, she worked in newspaper advertising and as a potter. Even though she had felt as a child that she had a call to the ministry, it was her second career, not her first. She became interested in becoming a chaplain because of the wide variety of activities that are possible in this form of ministry. She counsels and works closely with the prisoners, but she also spends time with such administrative tasks as setting up and supervising religious programs for the prisoners, doing public relations work, and recruiting and training volunteers. She must also allocate time to write budget reports required by the state. A paradox about being a prison chaplain is that while most Good Samaritans are rushing to help victims, the prison chaplain's ministry is to help the offender, who also needs healing.

Chaplain Woodruff's career satisfaction comes from her ability to see people change through their faith. Often she is able to see growth in moral development. Most of the time, this growth is slight or very gradual, but occasionally she is able to witness dramatic change. Chaplain Woodruff realizes that her form of ministry is not always valued by the system or even by those to whom she ministers. She advises people considering a career as a prison chaplain to work as volunteers first to see if they have an aptitude for this form of ministry.

The employment outlook is uncertain in this form of ministry. More and more people are being incarcerated, which means that money may be going for beds and food, and funding for prison chaplains may not be as high a priority.

Military Chaplain

As a result of the separation of church and state, chaplains in the United States are not drafted or compelled in any way to serve in the military. All military chaplains in this country are volunteers, and they always have been. They may serve short-term assignments or may have a lifetime career in the military.

Chaplains wear the uniform and have the rank and all the privileges and responsibilities of an officer but belong to an endorsing agency like a church. Since 1973, there have been female chaplains in the military. The job outlook is promising. There is a continuous need for military chaplains.

In peacetime, the job of a military chaplain is almost identical to that of a civilian pastor. However, in wartime, the chaplaincy becomes a crisis ministry on the battlefield.

Campus Chaplain

Being a chaplain on a college campus is a dynamic and exciting ministry. Many college students need remedial religious education. Often, chaplains deal with second and third generations of nonreligious students who also need considerable counseling.

College chaplain Fred Lamar entered this field because he always had a love for young people and higher education. He started out wanting to be a professor but learned that college teaching is often research oriented and would not give him the contact with students that he wanted. Chaplain Lamar holds several advanced degrees and explains that college chaplains are accorded more respect in the academic community if they have obtained higher degrees.

On the campus of DePauw University, where Chaplain Lamar works, the chaplain's program is based upon the belief that values, ethics, and faith are developed through reflection upon life experiences. Rather than preach to the students, Chaplain Lamar and the other chaplains started a program in 1975 that encouraged student participation in service experiences. Such experiences challenged them not only to lend a helping and caring hand but also to view the world from another's perspective, whether that of an abandoned inner-city child, a forgotten nursing home resident, or a third world peasant.

On campus, Chaplain Lamar coordinated the volunteer efforts of the college's twenty-four hundred students until 1994. The students gave time locally to Head Start and homes for the aged and to a program that rehabilitated homes in nearby urban areas. Students also worked with the poor and powerless throughout the United States and the world.

This work caused many students to change their majors and career choices. According to Chaplain Lamar, this experiential education created dedicated religious and political activists who understood that working for social justice is slow and difficult and who were willing to commit their lives to the cause.

In 1994, the volunteer program split from the chaplaincy to become a secular program under the direction of one of the school's other chaplains. This gave Chaplain Lamar time to focus more on religious matters.

Since the campus was becoming more diverse, he established the DePauw Interfaith Network, which let the different religious organizations on campus come together to share such religious activities as retreats and services. He believes that the students need to appreciate different religions as well as be securely grounded in their own faiths. In the summer, Chaplain Lamar has continued to work on volunteer service—an activity that he plans to continue after he retires.

Pastoral Counselors

Some people's problems are so serious and require so much counseling that pastors, ministers, rabbis, and chaplains do not have the training or time to give these people the in-depth help they require. Pastoral counselors have the training to provide this help. Some counselors have independent practices specializing in helping church members, while others are associated with a church or institution.

Women in Religious Careers

Although women are beginning to have more freedom in selecting careers in religion, they do not yet have total acceptance in every position within all religions. Religious communities are, however, becoming more attuned to the needs of the women in their orders.

Today, you can find women active in ministry work and playing a leadership role in providing communities with the social service programs they need. Women in religious careers are running day-care centers for children and shelters for the homeless. They are staffing the social work departments in hospitals, homes for the aged, treatment centers for disturbed children, and the youth ministry programs on college campuses. And more of these women are continuing their studies to earn master's and doctoral degrees in the social-service professions.

Deaconess

Deaconesses are officers of the church who help the ministers. The position of deaconess is open to women in only certain churches. The title *deaconess* dates back to biblical times, but the duties performed have changed through the ages. One constant is that deaconesses have always reached out to help the people who are easy to forget—the homeless, disabled, poor, and imprisoned.

Carleen F. Holtman felt a call to serve people in a hands-on capacity. The deaconess community offered her training that would provide opportunities to serve in a variety of settings. She was also attracted to the support that such a community or "order" offers. Career preparation included a bachelor's degree in theology as well as training through the Lutheran Deaconess Association (plus graduate courses on a nondegree basis).

Currently, Deaconess Holtman is serving in a Lutheran parish as the associate in ministry and is working in the areas of youth, education, worship, and visitation. This is her first professional call, and she was contacted about this position through the Lutheran Deaconess Association. She hopes to continue to work as a deaconess either in a parish setting or in social service. She also hopes to pursue a master's degree.

Churches have a great need for deaconesses. Currently, there are more positions available than there are deaconesses to fill them.

Deaconess Holtman sees the biblical story of the Good Samaritan as one about someone who wasn't afraid to touch the untouchable. She relates her job to being someone who can enable others to get on their feet and continue on their journey.

Minister

After earning a bachelor's degree in accounting and an M.B.A. in finance, Jane Voelkel worked as an accountant and a certified public accountant before entering the seminary. In high school, Jane knew that she wanted to be a minister, but she opted for a business career because her parents were accountants and she knew what accountants did.

Being an accountant was not a happy career choice for Jane, who found more satisfaction teaching Sunday school and being involved in her church's singles and youth programs. The thought of being an accountant for forty more years scared Jane, so she decided to pursue her calling and study for the ministry.

Being ordained a minister in the Methodist Church is a difficult six-year process. It requires many meetings and interviews, piles of paperwork, and a psychological examination to see if one is fit for the ministry. After ordination, Jane spent one year working as a chaplain in a state psychiatric hospital. Today, she is an associate pastor at a large suburban Methodist church that has one senior pastor and three associate pastors. She believes that future employment opportunities are excellent because there is a shortage of ministers.

Jane works with the adult ministry, and it seems to her that the most important part of this ministry is handling the unexpected. At times, she must find lodging for suddenly homeless families or console grieving families who have lost a loved one.

Fund-Raiser

It might not seem as if a job raising funds is an appropriate one for people who really want to help others. However, Debra Sheriff, who has a master of divinity degree, is a fund-raiser and would not agree with that assumption. Debra is finding career satisfaction through becoming acquainted with people in different settings, preaching occasionally, and helping people deal with money and stewardship issues. Debra feels that she is involved in what is known as the "ministry of hospitality"—helping people know that God and His church care about their needs, struggles, and comfort. Incidentally, fund-raising is one area in which women are very well accepted in churches and other church institutions.

Missionary Work

The classic conception of missionary work is serving in a remote area to bring a certain religion to the inhabitants. Today's missionaries are unlikely to encounter head-hunters or cannibals, as missionaries once did; however, there still are many parts of the world that exist in poverty.

There are at least three major categories of missionary service. The first is vocational mission, which includes people who are employed by a denomination or mission organization for an extended career. The need for this type of missionary work has gradually declined, as more and more of the responsibilities have been assumed by citizens of the nations where missionaries formerly carried out the work. Nevertheless, many denominations still maintain an overseas missionary presence. Although there is a reduced need for pastors and church-planting missionaries, there continue to be openings for people trained in medicine, education, agriculture, and a number of other fields.

Short-term mission service is rapidly growing in popularity. It is an inviting option for young people who wish to serve God and humanity overseas. Usually, a college degree is a prerequisite. Many denominations also stipulate a background in religious studies. Interested students should contact a mission or service agency to find out about current needs and specific requirements.

The major Roman Catholic and mainline Protestant denominational agencies usually provide their missionaries with a variety of support packages. Independent boards, on the other hand, often require candidates to raise their own support from North American congregations and individual donors. After a two- or three-year period, short-term missionaries may choose to end their service, although many return for one or several more terms.

Finally, volunteer mission service is often a second career following retirement. Many gifted educators and medical personnel have extended their careers by going overseas to work in places where their training and experience can meet ongoing needs. In many cases, these volunteers agree to work for minimal income.

Requirements for Missionary Work

If you are seriously considering a missionary position, you should ask yourself if you are able to do the following:

- learn new languages quickly
- adapt swiftly to new situations
- handle difficult living conditions
- adjust to primitive surroundings
- work as part of a team
- deal with separation from family and friends
- work without supervision
- be self-reliant under new circumstances
- adjust to different cultures

Finding a Position

You can find out more about opportunities in missionary work by investigating what local churches have to offer. More than half of today's thousands of missionaries are serving under the sponsorship of a church group. Appendix B lists agencies you can contact about opportunities for overseas service. In addition, you can get information about job openings and special training programs by writing to:

Overseas Personnel Office of Church World Service
475 Riverside Drive
New York, NY 10115
www.churchworldservice.org/employment

College Student Missionaries

During Birmingham-Southern College's interim term (the month of January), students have the option of spending a month in a service-learning project working with missionaries in developing countries. The program allows students to "love in deed" in areas far from campus. Since 1987, more than four hundred students have participated in these service-learning projects on four continents. The students have helped build a church in Bolivia, worked in the homes of Mother Teresa in Calcutta, worked in health-care and construction projects in Zimbabwe, developed a student camp for victims of Chernobyl in Belarus, and taught English in Honduras.

Prior to each January and in the semester following, students speak in local churches about the needs of the countries that they have visited and worked in. They try to provide a living link between the missionaries in the field and the local churches in northern Alabama.

Birmingham-Southern College is affiliated with the United Methodist Church, so all of these projects come from a Christian theological point of view. However, the projects are open to students regardless of their faiths, and every project is ecumenical in nature. The program is coordinated by the chaplain of the college, Dr. Stewart A. Jackson, who works closely with faculty and staff to provide the in-service learning.

Mission Aviation Fellowship (MAF)

The Mission Aviation Fellowship is a nondenominational Christian organization that operates a fleet of airplanes. It was started by Christian aviators who had served in World War II and saw the airplane as a means to spread the gospel throughout the world.

Originally, the major purpose of MAF was to conquer jungle barriers so that missionaries could reach primitive tribes. Because of the incredible needs of people throughout the world, MAF's ministry has expanded. Today, from forty-one bases in twenty-one countries, the 128 pilots of MAF fly to remote, developing areas supporting Christian missionaries, churches, medical and emergency services, education, and development. In some places, the need for MAF's service is even greater today than when the organization was founded. For example, in Zaire there were twice as many usable roads in the 1940s as there are now.

MAF planes fly nearly five million miles each year, landing on some three thousand airstrips—more than any major airline in the world. Worldwide, every four minutes, twenty-four hours a day, 365 days a year, an MAF flight takes off on a mission. These missions range from transporting an agricultural specialist who will teach an African farmer new ways to work depleted soil to flying food and other supplies in a cooperative relief effort with World Vision. Pilots may face grave danger. Once, before an MAF plane could land on an airstrip in Angola, local hospital missionaries had to check the field for land mines. These MAF flights were the hospital's only link to the outside world because the roads were too dangerous.

In *Flightwatch*, the newsletter of the MAF organization, the traits of pilots past and present are stated: pioneer, settler, innovator, and survivor. Besides being able to fly a plane, these pilots must have a minimum of two years of Bible school or college. And at most bases, they also must be mechanics. After being accepted into the program, the pilots must raise their own support and acquire the appropriate language skill for their field assignments.

Missionary Pilot. One of the resourceful and dedicated pilots of MAF is Jon Lewis. As a child living in Portugal with his missionary parents, Jon had heard of MAF. However, his plans when he was in graduate school studying physics were to pursue a career in the aerospace field, possibly as an astronaut. Then Jon went to Africa one summer and helped an uncle who was a missionary doctor. There he saw MAF in action, and his future was decided.

Jon saw in the MAF program the chance to combine his professional interest in aviation with his desire to help others. He returned home, graduated, and then worked at MAF in public relations until he got his pilot's license.

Jon has been an MAF pilot now for twenty years, eight of those years spent in Africa. Pilots typically spend three or four years overseas and then return home for six months to talk to churches and contributors about MAF.

Being an MAF pilot is quite different from being a commercial airline pilot in the United States. Pilots can only fly during daylight hours in Zaire. Typically, a pilot will fly four to six days a week and make from eight to fifteen stops in a day. Arriving at the hangar by 7:00 A.M., the pilot begins the day by making radio contact with all the bases to be visited to gather weather information and to learn of any emergencies requiring immediate attention. Sometimes a pilot learns that flights have been rescheduled.

While a pilot is in the air, a spouse or national worker will help out by keeping contact with the pilot and the bases by shortwave radio. The average flight lasts from twenty minutes to an hour. The landing strips are cut out of forest or grassland. The plane carries passengers, mail, and supplies.

Each flight meets very important needs, and no day is routine. One Christmas day, Jon heard a weak radio call for help from a research couple in the forest whose child was suffering a severe asthma attack. Jon took a doctor with him to help the child, who was then brought to a hospital where he recovered. While leaving the jungle airstrip, Jon saw that the only road, a single-lane dirt road, was blocked in both directions by a truck stuck in a mud hole with some fifteen trucks in each direction waiting to get by. The ill child could never have reached the hospital without the help of a pilot.

Saving lives is routine for MAF pilots. Reflecting on his twenty years as a pilot, Jon says that his job satisfaction lies in serving God in a unique way. Today, Jon is director of research at MAF, traveling around the world to look for new opportunities for MAF to provide service.

Religious Orders

The majority of religious orders are Roman Catholic, but the Episcopal and Lutheran churches also offer opportunities for service through religious orders. Most religious orders specialize in a certain service, such as taking care of the aged or teaching.

Members of all orders go through various stages before they take their final vows, which are customarily vows of poverty, chastity, and obedience. The members of each order lead their lives according to the teachings of the order's founder. Prayer and work are part of the tradition of all communities but are accented differently in orders that are primarily contemplative.

Today, many of the orders' traditions have changed. In the past, most orders adopted the style of dress worn at the time the order was founded. Now, although some orders allow members to wear secular clothes, others have kept the original style of clothing to help distinguish themselves as a group.

Members of most religious orders live in communities in a convent or monastery. Because some members need to be located closer to their work, they may live apart from the community but are still connected to the larger community for support.

Little Sisters of the Poor

The Roman Catholic order of the Little Sisters of the Poor was founded by Jeanne Jugan 150 years ago. She took the first step in founding this order when she carried an elderly blind woman from the street into her home and began to care for her. Today, there are more than four thousand members of Little Sisters of the Poor working in thirty countries around the world.

Members of the order enter knowing that their lives will be spent in humble service to the poor. They share their lives and their homes with the poor. They seek to cheer and console the hearts of the elderly and keep prayerful vigil beside them in their dying. The sisters collaborate in the many tasks necessary to make their homes truly homes for the elderly. They love, accept, and respect the people they serve. These Good Samaritans believe that the elderly living in their homes give more to them than they can ever give in return. The members of the Little Sisters of the Poor take a vow of hospitality in addition to their other vows.

The Community of the Transfiguration

The Community of the Transfiguration, an Anglican order for women, seeks to glorify God through a life dedicated to prayer and service. The community was founded in 1898 in Glendale, Ohio. The sisters first worked with the poor in Cincinnati and later founded Bethany Home for children in Glendale. The Community of the Transfiguration is an active order living in the monastic tradition. The daily schedule of the sisters includes time for work, meals, and recreation as well as time for prayer and worship.

Evangelism

There are many different career opportunities in religious organizations under the heading of evangelism. Some of these organizations are very large, like the Billy Graham Evangelistic Association, which is perhaps the best-known evangelical organization because of its coverage on television. Another organization, Campus Crusade for Christ International, began on the campus of UCLA in 1951 and now has more than sixteen thousand staff members and two hundred thousand volunteers spreading the claims of Christ through fifty different ministries. The largest ministry, however, is still that of the university campuses.

Both the Billy Graham Evangelistic Association and the Campus Crusade for Christ are para-church organizations. This means these organizations have no particular church affiliation but work alongside other churches in areas that are more difficult for local churches to impact. Staff members do not have to be ordained ministers, although many are. There are also positions requiring a wide variety of skills, including art, media, literary, and medical skills.

Music and Religion

In temples and churches across the country, music is an important part of religious worship—from the rhythm of African drums to the melodic voices of the Mormon Tabernacle Choir. Many large congregations employ directors of music to select music for services and direct choirs.

Cantor

A cantor is a unique combination of minister, music director, teacher, and chief soloist in a synagogue. While it is no longer considered unusual for women to be cantors, only about 30 percent of the cantors in the Reform movement of Judaism are women. Janice Roger became one of those women because of her desire to express her love of Judaism through music. As a cantor, Janice is involved with music at all liturgical services for the public and in all areas of the life cycle—birth, marriage, and death.

Janice's background includes a bachelor's degree in music and a bachelor's degree in sacred music from a seminary, where she studied music for the synagogue as well as philosophy and religion. Immediately upon graduation from the seminary, Janice became a cantor for a large congregation. Her career satisfaction comes from watching young people grow and develop Jewish identities. She believes a cantor most visibly helps members of congregations by elevating their spiritual lives through music. However, other aspects of this position are directly related to interpersonal needs at times of crisis, so there is a humanitarian side as well to being a cantor. Janice wants to continue her education in the area of counseling so that she can better serve her congregation.

The requirements for becoming a cantor are not consistent throughout the Reform movement. It may or may not be necessary to have attended a seminary. The employment outlook for cantors is good because there are many more positions than there are people to fill them.

Meeting Social Needs While Serving God

The various religious denominations help people with a variety of social needs and social problems. In the Judeo-Christian tradition, service to those in need, such as the poor, the aging, the widowed, the sick, and abandoned children, expresses true love of God.

Many of the human services programs that exist today first appeared in the monasteries and convents of the early churches. These programs, such as Lutheran Social Services, Jewish Community Services, and Catholic Charities, still contribute to the human needs of the community. There are also many newer groups, such as World Vision and the Salvation Army, serving people around the world through their love of God.

World Vision

In 1950, Dr. Bob Pierce, an evangelist serving as a war correspondent in Korea, founded World Vision to help the thousands of abandoned Korean War orphans. Today, World Vision offers help and hope to seventeen million underprivileged people through almost fifty-five hundred projects in more than eighty countries throughout Asia, Africa, the Americas, and Europe.

World Vision is the world's largest Christian international relief and development agency. Its workers can be found in places where natural disasters, war, and oppression have captured world attention, as well as in some of the most remote and forgotten corners of the earth. While the majority of World Vision projects are conducted overseas, projects also have been established in the United States. Working through local churches, these efforts have included low-cost housing for the urban and rural poor, job placement and training services, vocational training, leadership training for Native Americans, and programs to prevent drug abuse and counsel teenage mothers.

"Every project World Vision undertakes has two underlying principles," says Robert Seiple, president of the agency since 1987.

"One is that development is a partnership process where local people decide for themselves that they need to rise above poverty. World Vision then helps them meet their goals. The second is our belief that people everywhere—from the aborigines of Papua New Guinea to the homeless right in our own backyard—have physical, intellectual, and spiritual needs. We strive to meet all those needs. We want to feed people, educate people, and share our Christian motivation with them. But acceptance of our religious views has never been, nor ever will be, a condition for receiving our help. We offer assistance with no strings attached."

In 1987, as part of its mandate to assist the world's children, World Vision launched an aggressive campaign called "Child Survival and Beyond." This worldwide program has increased the agency's massive primary health-care effort, which includes inoculations against common childhood diseases, training in oral therapy and hygiene to prevent deaths by diarrheal diseases, education in breast-feeding, and regular growth monitoring to detect and prevent malnutrition.

Meanwhile, reaching beyond immediate needs, World Vision is providing for the future of the young lives that are saved by implementing water development projects, community health training, and, ultimately, economic development assistance. To accomplish its work throughout the world, World Vision uses a Christian staff and Christian volunteers.

The Salvation Army

So many people associate the Salvation Army with the officers, soldiers, and volunteers standing beside kettles ringing bells at Christmas, not realizing that the organization is actually a church, providing a multitude of services throughout the world. Currently, the Salvation Army serves close to ten million people a year in more than 109 countries and operates more than fifteen thousand centers in the United States.

The paramount purpose of the Salvation Army has always been to lead men and women into a proper relationship with God.

William Booth, the founder, recognized that in a congregation such as he faced in the slums of London, help toward physical, emotional, and social restoration must go hand in hand with spiritual rebirth. He believed in a "balanced ministry," where spiritual and physical support is united.

From Indonesia to India, Peru to Zambia, the Salvation Army wages war on poverty in home training centers, mobile clinics, hospitals and dispensaries, special schools, children's homes, day-care centers, refugee centers, kindergartens, and other facilities. In the United States, the Salvation Army serves the needy through emergency, year-round, and holiday programs, including such services as:

- food, clothing, and transitional housing assistance for families in crisis
- holiday meals for homeless or solitary people
- job training programs
- missing person's bureau
- relief for disaster victims
- residential chemical dependency treatment, medical services, and meals for people in need
- residential rehabilitation
- services for prisoners, parolees, and their families
- shelters for the homeless
- thrift stores
- visits to nursing homes, hospitals, and the homebound
- youth, family, and senior citizen programs

The basic unit of service is the corps community center, which is organized in a military manner, using military terms throughout. The centers are supervised by commissioned officers who are trained to proclaim the gospel and to serve as ministers, administrators, teachers, counselors, youth leaders, and musicians. The Salvation Army also employs lay personnel in many clerical, technical, and professional posts and uses volunteers.

American Jewish World Service

The American Jewish World Service was founded in 1985. The organization is dedicated to providing nonsectarian, humanitarian assistance and emergency relief to disadvantaged people in Africa, Asia, Latin America, and the Middle East as well as Russia and Ukraine. Through its skilled volunteers in the Jewish Volunteer Corps and long-term partnerships with grassroots nongovernmental organizations, the service supports and implements self-sustaining projects that respect the dignity, culture, and heritage of the people with whom it works. To learn about volunteer or international summer program opportunities, contact:

American Jewish World Service
45 West Thirty-Sixth Street, Tenth Floor
New York, NY 10018
www.ajws.org

The American Friends Service Committee

The American Friends Service Committee (AFSC) is a Quaker organization that includes people of various faiths who are committed to social justice, peace, and humanitarian service. Its work is based on the Quaker belief in the worth of every person and faith in the power of love to overcome violence and injustice. The AFSC was founded in 1917 to provide conscientious objectors with an opportunity to serve those in need instead of fighting during World War I. Today, the organization has hundreds of opportunities, ranging from weekend work camps to yearlong internships to two-year Peace Corps–type programs. Each month AFSC compiles a staff openings list that is available by writing to:

Office of Human Resources
American Friends Service Committee
1501 Cherry Street
Philadelphia, PA 19102
www.afsc.org

Visit the Quaker Information Center online for a long list of short, intermittent, midterm, and longer-term volunteer opportunities within the United States and abroad. You could find such opportunities as advocating for prisoners, encouraging spiritual growth in Moscow, working in after-school programs, and helping homeless people in soup kitchens and shelters.

Finding Your Niche

One does not have to be a minister, priest, rabbi, nun, deacon, deaconess, or monk to have a satisfying career combining religion and one's desire to be a Good Samaritan or humanitarian. Thousands of additional career opportunities exist. The teachers in religious schools, the counselors in church-run charities, the office and administrative staffs of religious groups, the doctors serving as missionaries, and all the people working in support positions in religious organizations are advancing the cause of humanity and their faith through their work.

Investigate Before Making the Commitment

Within different churches are many satisfying careers for Good Samaritans or humanitarians. Because the variety of careers is so great, you will need to read widely to discover the career that is right for you. The following books should help you in this task:

- *Yearbook of American and Canadian Churches*, available from the National Council of Churches, 475 Riverside Drive, Suite 880, New York, NY 10115, www.ncccusa.org.
- *The Catholic Almanac*, available from Our Sunday Visitor, 200 Noll Plaza, Huntington, IN 46750, www.osv.com.
- Various publications available from the Jewish Publication Society of America, 2100 Arch Street, Second Floor, Philadelphia, PA 19103, www.jewishpub.org.

These books are also available through bookstores.

Ready to Find a Job, but How?

Since one can be overwhelmed by the diversity of jobs in religious organizations, it is helpful to talk to a member of the clergy of the denomination that interests you for more specific career help. In addition, you can contact Intercristo, an organization that will match your background, skills, and interests with current openings in nonprofit Christian organizations.

Intercristo has information about thousands of full-time positions in more than 250 categories in nonprofit Christian organizations. You can contact these Christian career specialists for information by writing to:

Intercristo
19303 Fremont Avenue North
Seattle, WA 98133
www.intercristo.com

CHAPTER SIX

Volunteering: Make a Difference, Be the Difference

"No act of kindness, no matter how small, is ever wasted."
—**Aesop**

Why People Volunteer

Do people volunteer because they feel it is a civic responsibility, to feel good about themselves, or to make a difference in the world? The main reason most people volunteer is because they wish to make a difference in the world, but people also volunteer for these reasons:

1. They want to be helpful.
2. They want to improve the community.
3. They or a family member has a condition that a volunteer group supports.
4. They want to meet people.
5. They want to improve skills.
6. They need job experience.
7. They are bored.
8. Their therapist has suggested they do it.
9. Their probation officer has required it.
10. They are interested in the field in which they do volunteer work.

11. They need credit for a course they are taking.
12. They want to help prevent a governmental unit from spending too much money.
13. They want to learn what goes on inside a volunteer organization.
14. They are grateful for services received.
15. Their boss has recommended community involvement.
16. Volunteer activities enhance career resumes and college applications.

Join the Crowd

More than half of all Americans are volunteers. You usually don't see their names in headlines or their faces on television, but these hardworking Good Samaritans and humanitarians are making a difference in the lives of Americans in need. And there is no one description that is accurate for all volunteers, because volunteers range from investment bankers on Wall Street to homemakers in Tulsa and Boise. They are senior citizens with limited incomes, junior high school students, and people just like you, your family, your friends, and your neighbors.

Once a year, on Make a Difference Day, more than a million Americans reach out to help others through a variety of projects, from feeding the hungry to warming the homeless to teaching children. Volunteering in this country, however, is more than a one-day-a-year activity for many people who are connecting their lives to others on a regular basis.

The lives of millions of Americans are being touched by volunteers—from the inner-city single parent to the homeless person in a shelter. Religious and charitable organizations still play a major role in organizing the efforts of volunteers. However, employers and colleges are increasingly supporting volunteer groups. The causes all these groups support range from the traditional helping of the poor, hungry, and sick to new areas such as fighting drunk driving and improving the environment.

The roots of volunteering can be traced back to the major religions, especially Judaism and Christianity. The Bible offers many stories of how religious individuals have helped the needy. The origin of the term *Good Samaritan*, meaning one who unselfishly helps others, comes from the biblical story of the Samaritan who helped a man who had been beaten and robbed (Luke 10:29–37). The Bible also contains many admonitions to help others. In the Old Testament, Moses advises:

> At the end of every three years you shall bring forth all the tithe of your produce in the same year, and lay it up within your towns; and the Levite, because he has no portion of inheritance with you, and the sojourner, the fatherless, and the widow, who are within your towns, shall come and eat and be filled.
>
> —Deuteronomy 14:28–29

Volunteering has always been a part of the American culture and one of its great resources. In recent years, the number of volunteers has swelled, encouraged in part by President George H. W. Bush's "Points of Light Initiative." In speaking about his plan to promote volunteering, the president said, "This is what I mean when I talk of 'a thousand points of light'—that vast galaxy of people and institutions working together to solve problems in their own backyard." In 1997, President Clinton held a Presidents' Summit on Service in Independence Hall in Philadelphia. He was joined by every living former president or his representative and other prominent Americans. Their mission was to do nothing less than spark a renewed national sense of obligation, a new sense of duty, and a new season of service. President Clinton pointed out that the ethic of service must extend throughout a lifetime—not be a pursuit for just a week or month. Furthermore, he stressed that no one was ever too young or too old to serve.

As Americans begin a new century, we are not relying on the government to solve all problems. Instead, volunteers of all ages and from all walks of life are discovering their ability to make a difference. Peyton Manning, quarterback for the Indiana Colts, created PeyBack to promote success among disadvantage youth. Reggie White, defensive end for the Green Bay Packers, created the Urban Hope Foundation to tackle problems of the inner-city poor. Captain Scott O'Grady, who eluded the Bosnian Serbs for six days after being shot down by a surface-to-air missile, volunteers time at elementary schools, youth detention centers, prisons, and hospitals. Bruce Springsteen and Sting have given benefit concerts to increase awareness of political oppression and destruction of the rain forest.

Are You Ready to Volunteer?

Everyone has something special to contribute as a volunteer, whether it is technical skills, time, concern, enthusiasm, or all of these things. While people may be motivated to serve as volunteers for different reasons, good volunteers possess these five traits:

- flexibility
- initiative
- humor
- commitment
- patience

While volunteering can be an extremely rewarding activity, it is not for everyone. Wanting to make a difference is important, but you must have realistic expectations. You are not going to eliminate all poverty, teach everyone to read, stop all drug abuse, or keep all young people in school. But you will be rewarded by knowing that you are making a small contribution to making the world a better place for others. You are probably ready to serve as a volunteer if you can answer yes to most of the following questions:

1. Do I want to volunteer?
2. Am I a flexible person? Can I adjust my thinking to time and place?
3. Am I willing to serve others in the way they want to be served?
4. Do I handle change and stress well?
5. Do I relate well to other people?
6. Am I the independent type? Can I work well on my own?
7. Am I capable of showing initiative?
8. Can I laugh at myself and see the funny side in an uncomfortable situation?
9. Can I accept cultural differences?
10. Can I work as a team member?

Finding the Right Fit

There are thousands of ways and places to volunteer. The difficult task is deciding which project is right for you. When you are considering a project, *Volunteer*, a comprehensive guide to voluntary service in the United States and abroad, suggests that you consider the following points in order to evaluate the project:

1. Who is the sponsoring organization? What is its affiliation? Although many of the programs you'll come across may not sound familiar, they may be affiliated with larger entities. Be sure to find out exactly who you'll be serving.
2. What is the financial situation of the sponsoring organization? Is it tax exempt? How does it finance itself? What role, if any, will you be expected to play in its fundraising activities? Remember that you can always ask for the organization's annual report in order to get an accurate account of its finances.
3. What do former volunteers have to say about the program? Any worthwhile organization is willing to give the names of

former participants so that you can contact them yourself and ask for a firsthand report on their experiences. The value of this kind of contact cannot be overemphasized.

If you are going to make a long-term commitment that requires you to live in another area in the United States or abroad, then you will need to consider these additional points:

1. What kind of provision will be made for health insurance while you are in service? Some programs provide insurance; others require participants to provide their own. Either situation may be acceptable, but be sure to know which applies.
2. What kind of staff supervision is provided in conjunction with the program? This varies enormously among programs, and, like the previous insurance question, it is something that should be clearly spelled out before you begin service.
3. If you have a student loan, is it possible to have payments deferred while you are in service? There are no loan deferments available for volunteer work if your loan was made after July 1, 1993, but it might be possible to receive a deferment for economic hardship.
4. What will be the living arrangements? Obviously, you can't expect luxury, but it is best to be prepared for whatever is coming. Ask the organization to be specific about the range of possible accommodations. Here, too, former participants can be enormously helpful.
5. What happens if you can't complete your term of service? Although you hope it won't happen, it can. You should know how the organization will react.
6. How does the organization prepare its participants for the experience? Carefully review any orientation materials or plans, and look at any written material with a critical eye. Trust your instincts on these things. You must feel confi-

dent about your choice of sponsoring organization before you begin service, just as the sponsors must feel absolutely confident about their choice of you.

7. If the position is overseas, what are the necessary visas or other official papers that you'll need? How are these papers to be obtained? What about health regulations—are there any necessary vaccinations or other precautions for the part of the world you'll be going to?

State Offices of Volunteerism

Almost every state has an office of volunteerism, which provides volunteers and organizations with a wide range of information. Appendix C has a list of these state offices.

In Arkansas, the Division of Volunteerism promotes and supports volunteerism in the private, nonprofit, and government sectors as a means of solving problems for all Arkansans. The division offers the following services:

- provides resources, technical assistance, program consultation, and research to statewide volunteer programs and nonprofit organizations through a resource center
- administers and monitors grants and provides training opportunities for national service programs
- provides volunteers to help families moving from welfare to independence
- holds an annual conference for managers of volunteers and volunteer programs and professionals in the nonprofit sector
- recruits, screens, and refers prospective volunteers to Department of Human Services division
- publishes a magazine and a quarterly newsletter with information about volunteer programs
- provides organizations with technical assistance on all aspects of volunteer management
- holds training and workshop programs

- assists with the formation and support of volunteer centers
- provides recognition for volunteers and volunteer organizations
- provides publicity for volunteer events

Financial Aspects of Being a Volunteer

There are a number of tax benefits available to volunteers. Volunteers may deduct unreimbursed out-of-pocket expenses directly related to their volunteer service if they itemize deductions. A general rule is that, when deducting volunteer-related expenses, organizations or companies operated for profit do not qualify. Examples of the types of expenditures that volunteers may deduct on their tax returns include:

- bus and cab transportation expenses
- parking costs and tolls
- the cost and expenses of upkeep of special uniforms
- telephone bills
- supplies purchased to perform volunteer duties
- automobile mileage and expenses for gas and oil
- dues, fees, or assessments made to a qualified organization
- noncash contributions of property (e.g., clothing, books, household items, equipment)

Individuals or couples who volunteer as foster parents may deduct unreimbursed expenses paid to provide foster care. These expenses must be amounts spent in support of the children placed in their homes by a charitable organization.

Volunteers may deduct automobile expenses at a standard rate per mile or on an actual expense basis. Volunteers may not deduct general automobile repair and maintenance expenses. Good record keeping for transportation-related costs is a must for volunteers who intend to claim automobile-related deductions.

More detailed information on deductions can be obtained from the Internal Revenue Service. To make it easy to keep track of expenses incurred in volunteering, you should use a form like that in Figure 1.

Figure 1. Volunteer Tax Record-Keeping Form

Name of Volunteer _____

Organization (complete a separate sheet for each organization for which you volunteered) _____

Date and Nature of Expense
   (bus fare, mileage, phone calls, supplies)   Amount

_____ $ _____
_____ $ _____
_____ $ _____
_____ $ _____
_____ $ _____
_____ $ _____
_____ $ _____
_____ $ _____
_____ $ _____
_____ $ _____
_____ $ _____
_____ $ _____
_____ $ _____
_____ $ _____
_____ $ _____

Signature of Supervisor

_____

Prepared by VOLUNTEER—The National Center, 1111 North Nineteenth Street, Suite 500, Arlington, VA 22209

Educational Loan Deferment and Cancellation Information

Individuals with Stafford Loans and Perkins Loans may receive deferments for up to three years while doing volunteer work if the loan was made before July 1, 1993. During this time, payments are not required and interest does not accrue.

If your volunteer service causes you an economic hardship, as defined by the holder of your student loan, you may be eligible for a loan deferment of up to three years providing the loan was made after July 1, 1993. You must formally request a deferment through the procedures established by the holder of your loan, and you must continue making payments until you're notified that the deferment has been granted. Those participating in an Ameri-Corps program will be eligible to have past loans deferred and the accrual interest paid upon completion of service.

If you serve with the Peace Corps, AmeriCorps*VISTA, Ameri-Corps*NCCC, or AmeriCorps*State and Direct, up to 70 percent of a Perkins loan may be cancelled. Also, if you are employed in certain designated jobs in education, law enforcement, and medicine, all or part of your Perkins loan may be eligible for cancellation depending on the date the loan was made. Check with the school that made this loan to have your questions about cancellation and deferment answered.

Commitment to Volunteering

Mother Teresa once said, "The test at the end of life is not what you do, it is how much of yourself, how much love you put into what you do." Volunteering is evidence of caring. It is a personal effort to put a dent in today's problems—homelessness, hunger, AIDS, poverty, inadequate health care, unsafe water, polluted air, and illiteracy.

Millions of Americans are taking steps as volunteers to make life better for others. They are serving in child-care centers, shaping young lives. They are visiting and caring for the elderly. Listening ears and plenty of understanding are available for troubled teens. Hope is being extended to refugees from political violence and oppression. Indeed, volunteering is alive and well in America. The candy stripers in the hospital, the Marines collecting toys for tots, the Red Cross workers at a blood drive, and the volunteer firefighters are all giving their time and their hearts to others.

Volunteers are needed everywhere. There are thousands of opportunities for volunteering that people are fitting into their daily schedules. And they are making a true commitment, because the average volunteer is serving almost five hours a week.

To most people, volunteering means giving a portion of their time each week. For some, it actually means bringing careers to a halt or delaying the start of careers to spend all their time as volunteers. For many, volunteering becomes a full-time job after retirement. And there are those who spend their vacations serving as volunteers.

Whether you live in a small community or a large metropolitan area, opportunities exist for you to volunteer your services. There are well-known and small, unknown niches of society needing volunteers. One of the easiest ways to find out about volunteering in your community is by contacting the local United Way organization. Also, newspapers often print the names of organizations needing volunteers.

The Spirit of Volunteerism

Good Samaritans and humanitarians serve as volunteers in organizations throughout America. The following brief stories about volunteers and their organizations will show you some of the thousands of opportunities available for volunteers.

Volunteerism as a Way of Life

Jan Snell has been an active volunteer for more than thirty years. Her introduction to volunteering was playing the piano for Sunday church services while she was in junior high school—an activity that she continued through her freshman year of college. By the time Jan was in high school, her commitment to volunteering became a five-day-a-week, eight-hour-a-day job during the summer. Jan worked at a veteran's hospital as a candy striper, and her volunteer work reinforced her desire to become a nurse.

Throughout the years, whether Jan was going to school, working, or raising a family, volunteering has always played a very important role in her life. Jan has been active in scouting, the Crossroads Rehabilitation Center, Meals on Wheels, and her children's schools. Within many of these organizations, she has chaired committees and been a board member. Today, her time commitment varies from two to thirty hours a week. Jan explains her commitment to volunteering by saying that she has been blessed with a rich and satisfying life and that she adheres to the biblical idea that those who receive much are expected to give much in return.

A Young Volunteer

Sarra Jo Todd is one the legions of unsung volunteers. Although she is only fourteen years old, Sarra spends much of her free time volunteering. As a member of Royal Roofers, she roofs houses and tackles other projects of the group. Sarra has helped rehabilitate houses for low-income families and has visited the elderly and done household chores for them. This young Good Samaritan is truly a devoted volunteer. During the winter months, she may work on volunteer projects on Friday evenings and all day on Saturdays and Sundays. In the summer, her volunteer time extends to eight hours a day, five days a week. Why does she spend her time volunteering when she could be going to movies or watching television? Sarra volunteers because she wants to help her community. She does not like looking at vacant lots with weeds and trash; she wants her neighborhood to look nice.

Sarra has won the Youth Volunteer of the Year Award in Indianapolis, Indiana. She was selected for this honor from a total of more than four hundred volunteers in the Youth as Resources organization. Royal Roofers receives funds from Youth as Resources, a community-based organization for young people ages ten to twenty who discover community needs and develop projects to fill these needs. The program director for Youth as Resources describes Sarra as a real motivator for the other youths in her group, a special person who has the leadership quality that makes an excellent volunteer.

Hearing the Call to Serve

As far back as she can remember, Abby Henkel enjoyed volunteering. She remembers as a kid going with her church group to serve at a local women's shelter. In high school Abby served on the Action Board and was a cochair of the Marketing Committee for Youth as Resources (YAR), a United Way organization that provides grant opportunities for youth-driven service projects. Through high school and now, in college, she participated in her church's yearly youth Habitat for Humanity trip. During these trips she would spend a week in another state building a house for a family.

Abby feels she has always gained something from her service experiences, which is why she keeps looking for new volunteer experiences. It's never for any sort of monetary benefit. She finds it very inspiring and fulfilling to see the looks on the faces of new home owners or to see the projects that youth design and implement based on the resources gained from YAR. It is experiences like these that have led Abby to a life dedicated to serving others.

Now as a young college student, Abby has served two summer terms with AmeriCorps*Vista. She worked with the Indianapolis Greenways cleaning up bike trails and painting murals. Abby's most recent service was with Literacy PLUS helping to develop a literacy program for homeless adults in Indianapolis at the Horizon House, a day center for the homeless. She has learned about the challenges of helping a nonprofit organization begin a new program. She gained experience in planning, marketing, networking, and fund-raising. This experience has helped Abby hone her own skills and see where she can excel. By serving with Ameri-Corps*VISTA, she has learned how to combine different talents and abilities to better serve the people who need the most help.

Damien Center: An Organization for Persons Affected by AIDS

The Damien Center is a comprehensive center for AIDS education, counseling, and support. It serves those with HIV, as well as their friends and families, through its client support system.

In August of 1988, Alan Edwards discovered he had AIDS. He returned to his home to be with family and became involved with the Damien Center as a result of a call to an AIDS hotline number. Once Alan saw the number of Damien Center clients with AIDS, especially the babies and young children, he decided he didn't have the time to feel sorry for himself. He became involved in helping others with AIDS and went through the Damien Center volunteer-training program.

Until his death, Alan was a full-time volunteer at the Damien Center. He worked fifty to sixty hours a week free of charge, which saved the center $25,000 a year. Alan wore many hats in his role as a full-time volunteer. He worked with client services, was a consultant to the Midwest AIDS Training Educational Center, and was a member of two needs task forces and a volunteer committee. He spent time speaking to the public to educate people about AIDS. To raise money for the food pantry at the center, Alan made buttons that said "Silence Equals Death." In addition, Alan created a memory book, a book with pictures of center members who had died of AIDS, something he started so that people wouldn't forget those who were gone.

Alan was willing to do whatever needed to be done around the center—from making coffee to cleaning up. His time as a volunteer entitled him to carry business cards showing he was a staff member who represented the Damien Center. Alan felt that he knew the needs of persons with AIDS and tried to help make life easier for them. He hoped that there would be a volunteer to help him when he needed one, and there was.

Community Volunteers

Helping the needy in Contra Costa County in Northern California is truly a full-time job for Peggy Scott. One day a week she volunteers at Loaves and Fishes, a soup kitchen that feeds the homeless. Then she spends a day helping the homeless at Shelter Inc.'s rental assistance program. Serving on the boards of both organizations also fills her days. In addition, she spends considerable time in fund-raising endeavors for Loaves and Fishes, which serves more than 125,000 meals a year on the small budget of $300,000 plus donations of food. To get the needed money, Peggy is continuously applying for grants. Peggy has chosen to help the less fortunate not only because of their great need, but because she believes in the Christian tenet of helping others.

When Bob Mitchell retired, he went to an agency to learn about volunteer opportunities in his city. The needs were so great that he elected to work at several agencies. Two days a week, he is a driver for Red Cross, taking people who don't have transportation to hospitals and clinics. Then once a week he has a Meals-on-Wheels route that takes him to the homes of the same people each week. In addition, Bob does glaucoma screening for the Society to Prevent Blindness and drives a bookmobile and dispenses books to children in low-income neighborhoods. Bob believes that you must do something worthwhile for yourself as well as the community.

Hospital Volunteers

With hospitalization becoming increasingly expensive, the role of the hospital volunteer becomes even more important. Not only do volunteers provide important patient services, but they also reduce staff costs. Volunteers take patients to their rooms, staff gift shops, deliver flowers and mail, run book and magazine carts, provide information, and do innumerable other tasks.

Kristin Newby's grandfather, Maurie Copan, convinced her to try volunteering at a hospital after he became a hospital volunteer himself. This inspired her to work every Saturday for about five hours—handing out menus, helping the patients fill them out, and collecting them—while she was in high school. When she had a day off from school, Kristin accompanied her grandfather to the hospital if he was volunteering that day.

Before becoming a volunteer, Kristin wanted to pursue a music-related career. Volunteering helped her decide to become a nurse. Serving as a volunteer is an excellent way for young people to explore career possibilities. And when families volunteer together, it brings a special closeness, such as Kristin and her grandfather have enjoyed.

Rebecca Mau is another student who sees a career in medicine in the future. Someday, she would like to be a doctor; however, today she is busy as a volunteer, sterilizing surgeon's tools and everything from rubber bands to safety pins that will be used in a hospital. In talking about her volunteer work, Rebecca says, "I can learn as much as I want or I can just get down there and do the job. I choose usually to ask questions." She has already had the chance to see an appendectomy and has the opportunity to move up to the volunteer position of nurse's assistant next summer. Rebecca's volunteer work is not limited to the hospital. She also volunteers with Tree of Hope, which lets her take one or two underprivileged children out to do "fun" stuff, such as movies, baseball games, and bowling. This project makes her appreciate all the advantages that she has enjoyed. Besides volunteering, Rebecca works forty hours a week and is a member of the National Honor Society, illustrating that busy Good Samaritans can integrate volunteering into their schedules.

Corporate Volunteers

It is now possible for Good Samaritans and other humanitarians to participate in volunteer activities through their workplaces. Corporations are increasingly establishing formal programs to encourage employees to serve as volunteers. Some corporations let employees serve as volunteers during work hours, and a few even give their employees paid leave to work in nonprofit organizations. The rewards that corporations receive from supporting volunteer activities include an improved public image and increased work satisfaction from their employees.

The Harris Bank in Chicago has a volunteer council, composed of representatives from all areas of the bank, which facilitates, coordinates, and promotes volunteerism. The employees on the council organize a volunteer project each month and recruit participants. Some of the projects are annual, such as the school supply drive in the fall, in which employees contribute, organize, and distribute supplies to local schools, and the Easter basket project, during which employees put together baskets for nonprofit organizations. Many of the projects are one-day events, such as the annual March of Dimes Walkathon. Others are ongoing, such as tutoring or serving on the board of a nonprofit organization. In addition, Harris has a "Dollars for Doers" program that supports the volunteer efforts of its employees. Under this program, the bank awards monetary grants to qualified nonprofit organizations for which a Harris employee actively volunteers.

The Target Company, which has upscale discount retail stores across the country, supports volunteerism by having a Good Neighbor Committee in each store. These committees focus on what events are occurring in their communities and select one or more each month as a volunteer activity. Then the group goes out into the community to do such things as clean parks and riverbeds, participate in walkathons, and volunteer at senior citizen centers.

The Hewlett-Packard Company, located in the heart of Silicon Valley in California, designs, manufactures, and services electronic products and systems for measurement, computing, and communication. Besides being a leader in the computer industry, the company avidly supports education through its employee volunteer and product gift program. Each employee volunteer receives up to four hours a month of paid time to participate in Hewlett-Packard's school volunteer program. Also, employees who wish to donate company equipment to schools only have to pay 25 percent of the cost. The goals of the company's education program are to improve children's achievement in science and mathematics, to increase the number of women and minorities studying and teaching science and mathematics, and to ensure that all children are ready to learn when they start school. This has led to such volunteer activities as Bill Knight volunteering one day a week to be Mr. Science at an elementary school in Corvallis, Oregon, and Hewlett-Packard e-mail mentors working with middle school students in Atlanta, Georgia.

One day Randy Wells, a loan officer at the University of Illinois Employees Credit Union, realized he was bored with just eating lunch during his lunch hour. He asked the Champaign, Illinois, United Way if he could help others somehow. Yes, they said, and the service that needed help most was Meals on Wheels, a program that delivers hot lunches to the elderly and other shut-ins.

Randy went back to his office and told coworkers about the program. Many others were also intrigued, so together they asked the president of the credit union whether he objected to this extracurricular activity. The president was so enthusiastic that he offered the use of the company car one day a week for the program. Meals on Wheels, though, really needed help every weekday, so the employees decided to use their own cars the other days. For seven years, two employees went on the Meals on Wheels route each day. About twenty-four employees participated in the program, so each volunteer traveled the ninety-minute route twice a month. The group then became involved in the Catholic Services lunch program, helping prepare and serve lunch, and is now searching for another volunteer activity.

Mennonite Voluntary Service (MVS)

Mennonite Voluntary Service volunteers respond to crises, both subtle and obvious, every day. The organization is committed to bringing about changes in society and its structures. Peace and justice workers educate people about nonviolence and confront oppressive powers and structures. Organizers help neighbors unite to take control of the welfare of their communities. Assignments are in a broad range of fields, and many entry-level positions are available. Areas in which volunteers currently serve include:

- business services
- child care
- church-community work
- community development
- economic development
- education
- emergency aid
- health services
- housing rehabilitation
- legal aid
- mental health
- peacemaking
- prison work
- senior services
- tutoring
- welfare rights advocacy
- youth work

For most MVS participants, volunteering is a full-time job; a two-year commitment is strongly urged. These volunteers usually live together in units with three to twelve other members. They may be single or married. Some volunteers come from Mennonite backgrounds, but nearly one-third of those serving do not. MVS provides an allowance that supports volunteers in a lifestyle of realistic simplicity. Health care and transportation to and from assignments are also provided. The units arrange to meet local transportation needs of their members.

Scott Bergen was one of MVS's youngest volunteers as a recent high school graduate from Calgary, Alberta. He joined MVS because he wanted to try something new and saw this as a good time to sort out career goals. His love for children made him a good candidate for Friendship Day Care in Hutchinson, Kansas, where he cared for eighteen rambunctious preschoolers. For Scott, working in the day-care center proved to be tougher than he'd thought, but it "showed me what's out there, broadened my horizons," he said. For the first time, Scott had to address issues such as child abuse and neglect.

Phil and Norma Duerken are MVS members who served at the Pleasant Valley Outdoor Center (PVOC) in Woodstock, Illinois. PVOC was built in a setting where the economically disadvantaged could enjoy life, where scars could heal, and where issues could be discussed in safety. Located on 460 acres of woodlands, ponds, prairies, and marshes, PVOC served as a perfect place for children to develop a better understanding of themselves, others, and their environment.

During the summer, busloads of children came from the inner city of Chicago to stay at PVOC for twelve days. Phil led the children in nature awareness activities, such as day hikes, games that require awareness of nature through the use of all the senses, and nighttime hikes and stargazing. His reward was acceptance from children of all races and their outpouring of love. Norma helped the children express themselves through arts and crafts. She saw children come reluctantly to her program and leave with pride in what they could create.

During the fall and spring, school groups from the suburbs came to use PVOC for their environmental education classes. This was a wonderful opportunity for children who had no chance to experience the silence, space, and colors of nature or to feel the openness of the prairie, the silence of a forest, or a starlit night without streetlights and cars. For Phil and Norma, working at PVOC was a "stretching" experience, allowing them to see a different world. Today, Norma is a Mennonite pastor, continuing with Phil to be an active Good Samaritan.

Information about MVS can be obtained by contacting:

Mennonite Voluntary Service
722 Main Street
PO Box 347
Newton, KS 67114

Mennonite Voluntary Service
1251 Virginia Avenue
Harrisonburg, VA 22802

Mennonite Voluntary Service
500 South Main Street
PO Box 370
Elkhart, IN 46515

You can also obtain information at www.mennonitemission.net.

Habitat for Humanity International

Habitat for Humanity is a nonprofit, grassroots organization committed to eliminating poverty housing from the world and making decent shelter a matter of conscience. Founded in 1976 by Millard and Linda Fuller as a response to the worldwide housing crisis, Habitat's efforts have made decent, affordable housing a reality for more than sixty thousand families worldwide.

By having affluent and poor people work together in equal partnership, Habitat hopes to build new relationships and a sense of community as well as new houses. Homes are constructed by volunteers and prospective home owners using donated materials and funds. Homes are then sold at cost, with a long-term, no-interest mortgage. Home owners are selected without regard to race or religion.

As a Habitat volunteer, you could serve in the United States, Canada, Latin America, Africa, the Middle East, Asia, the Pacific Islands, Europe, or the Caribbean. Habitat welcomes men and women, married and single, retired, midcareer, and just out of school. In North America, volunteers need to be at least fourteen years old to do construction work. For international sites, volunteers need to be twenty-one or older.

Local Volunteers. By far, most volunteers who work with Habitat for Humanity do so in their local communities. There are more than thirteen hundred affiliates in the United States, and every affiliate has one or more projects. Each of the affiliates welcomes donations of time and skills by concerned volunteers from the surrounding area. If you are interested, simply contact your local affiliate and ask how you can help—whether it is for one day or longer.

Orientation to the Habitat program is given locally, and whatever training you need is provided on the job site. Local affiliates have some need of full-time volunteers who have specific skills in construction, administration, office work, and development.

In 1987, Warren and Jean Perney decided to become part of the solution to providing housing for low-income working families. They were members of a group that formed a Habitat for Humanity affiliate in Indianapolis, Indiana. Warren, a retiree, was elected president. He immediately began putting in sixty-hour weeks, drumming up support for the program during the day and recruiting volunteers at night. Jean, who was still working full-time, became his valued assistant. They ran the affiliate's office out of their home, even using their home as a temporary warehouse for donated materials.

Once Warren's term as president was over, he was out of a job but not out of work. Both he and his wife worked with other volunteers to find enough sponsors and workers to build fifteen homes in one week in August 1991. Today, this affiliate has constructed close to one hundred homes, and Jean is now recruiting families for Habitat homes.

Headquarters Volunteers. Volunteers working at headquarters in Americus, Georgia, usually stay a minimum of three months; however, terms of a year or longer are preferred. At headquarters, Habitat's work in North America and around the world is coordinated. Volunteers with office skills are needed, as well as those who can provide help in hospitality, graphic arts, photography, printing, and language translation. Volunteers may stay in furnished housing with utilities and household supplies provided. Insurance and a weekly food stipend are also available.

The headquarters also hosts one- and two-week work camps for senior high school, college-aged, and adult groups. Volunteers work in office and construction settings and share in field trips and local activities.

While in college in North Dakota, Annette Martel was introduced by some of her friends to Habitat for Humanity. One of the highlights of her years in college was participating in the organization's Collegiate Challenge spring break trips, during which she gained most of her construction skills. For a week, Annette and her college friends would travel to another area of the United States to work on a construction project. She especially appreciated this opportunity to see different cultures and to work with home owners. By spring of her junior year, she was elected to the board of directors of the Red River Valley Habitat for Humanity, serving on the publicity and construction committees and becoming actively involved in the organization's decisions.

Annette became so hooked on the activities of Habitat that she is now completing an internship at headquarters. Her job ties in with her major in communications, as she is working in the audiovisual department, which oversees the production of informational and promotional videos. She also handles loads of media requests and pitches in to do clerical work when needed. Once her internship is completed, Annette plans to work as a volunteer at headquarters for a year in the media relations department. She considers working in public relations for a large nonprofit organization, specifically Habitat for Humanity, an incredible opportunity.

Annette now works eight hours a day Monday through Friday. This leaves time for construction activities on Saturdays, when she can fit them in. She lives in community housing provided by Habitat with what she describes as a neat mix of people, from recent college graduates to retirees. Because her stipend for living expenses is only $56.25 a week, she and her fellow volunteers have to be creative in devising recreational activities.

For Annette, Habitat has been a win-win situation. By helping to eliminate poverty housing and improving the lives of many people, her own life is more fulfilled. Habitat has changed her perspective on life as she has seen how people with resources (money, materials, or talents) can help fill a great need when they work together and receive rewards far more valuable than those they have donated. That's what volunteering means to her.

International Volunteers. At locations in one hundred participating countries in Africa, the Middle East, Asia and the Pacific, Europe, Canada, and Latin America and the Caribbean, volunteers serve three-year stints. These Habitat volunteers must have experience in administration, construction, or community organizing. Applicants who have proficiency in a foreign language or have lived overseas previously are preferred.

Before going abroad, volunteers spend four weeks in a training program at headquarters. Then for one month after training, the volunteers share the vision of Habitat while seeking financial and prayer support for their term abroad. When they are abroad, full health insurance, housing, a monthly stipend, and travel expenses are covered. At the international sites, the volunteers are eventually expected to work themselves out of a job by enabling local people to assume the administration of the project.

Habitat also has international work camps. These camps offer the chance to work side by side with national and international partners building houses for a one- to four-week period. For these work camps, groups of eight to ten people, eighteen years and older, pay their own way to visit and share in the building at an international project.

The Carters and Habitat. Throughout his term as president of the United States, Jimmy Carter was deeply committed to social justice, peace, and basic human rights. When he and his wife, Rosalynn, left the White House, they began searching for new ways to continue working toward these ideals. The Carters found that Habitat for Humanity provided a tangible demonstration of the ideals they valued. The former president describes his involvement in Habitat projects as "exciting, somewhat controversial, inspirational, challenging, unpredictable, extremely worthwhile, highly successful, and international in scope."

The Carters say they have benefited from their involvement with Habitat in many ways. "These work experiences have let us learn a lot about ourselves and about each other," Carter says. He also says Rosalynn has "never looked more beautiful than with a hammer in her hand and sweat on her brow," while working on a Habitat house. Since the Carters became active supporters of Habitat for Humanity in 1984, the organization has more than quadrupled in size. For information about volunteering, write:

Habitat for Humanity
121 Habitat Street
Americus, GA 31709
www.habitat.org

You can visit the Habitat website to learn about how to get involved, read true stories of volunteers, and find out more about how Habitat works.

Lutheran Volunteer Corps (LVC)

The Lutheran Volunteer Corps seeks to help those who are oppressed. Volunteers live in a community with other volunteers and explore a simplified lifestyle. They work in direct service organizations like shelters, soup kitchens, after-school programs, and health clinics in five metropolitan areas. In addition, they advocate for more just policies at local, state, and national levels. Volunteers must make a one-year commitment. If they wish, they may also spend a second year at the same placement or at a different one.

For more information about LVC, contact:

Lutheran Volunteer Corps
1226 Vermont Avenue NW
Washington, DC 20005
www.lutheranvolunteercorps.org

As part of the LVC, Diane Docis served as a volunteer at My Sister's Place (MSP), a shelter for battered women and their children. Through her work, Diane feels she developed a bond with all women who are oppressed. As a result of her service at MSP, Diane now believes that as long as a woman is beaten every fifteen seconds in the United States, she is not free, and neither are her niece or her sisters.

Diane continued to work at the shelter after her first year of service. She was not selflessly serving, she says, but working for justice for herself, for women she knew, and for those she would never meet. Diane believes that justice issues are interconnected. She saw the proof of this statement when she answered a hotline call from a woman who had been abused physically and psychologically for ten years. This woman had finally decided to leave her husband, only to be faced with homelessness, unemployment, and no child care.

Diane feels that people's strength and determination to survive is incredible. She has been amazed and inspired by numerous formerly battered women whose courage and inner reserves have saved their lives. Now when she is discouraged, she gains hope thinking of these people—Lillian, Sharon, Monica, and the many others.

Diane also feels that one person can make a difference. So often during her first year of service, she felt overcome by the immensity of injustice and felt powerless to effect change. Then she would hear a resident at the shelter convincing a hurt, frightened newcomer that nothing she did made her deserve to be battered, that the victim was a brave woman who now was safe. Or she would see a volunteer on a Saturday morning gather together a lively group of children from MSP for a picnic in the park. Or someone would send a donation at just the right time, enough to pay for a week's worth of food. At these times, Diane would realize the importance of what one person can do. She also learned that support from others is essential to maintaining one's efforts in the struggle for justice, and that balance in integrating work and play, body and spirit is vital to a whole, healthy life.

Volunteer Vacations

Instead of going to Yosemite National Park just to enjoy the scenery, vacation volunteers can join a conservation crew. And instead of going to New York City to circle Staten Island on the ferry, visitors can help the homeless in Harlem. And on a trip to Africa, a safari to see the animals is exciting, but planting crops feeds hungry people.

More and more Americans are discovering volunteer vacations. What's more, they are coming back from these vacations feeling more refreshed and satisfied than they would from sightseeing and sunbathing vacations.

From one week to an entire summer, a volunteer vacation is an adventure that benefits others. There is no shortage of volunteer projects. Thousands of projects are available throughout the year, with enough diversity to tap the skills and resources of every volunteer. For example, the U.S. Forest Service is usually in search of volunteers who are willing to get dirty and are physically able to do the hard work of planting young trees. And international work camps are places where real needs are met. Small groups of people from many countries come together to work on projects in different nations. Volunteers not only get to work on a project, they also get to know other volunteers and people in the community. If you are interested in a volunteer vacation, you can find information about many projects in the book *Volunteer Vacations: Short-Term Adventures That Will Benefit You and Others* by Bill McMillon, published by Chicago Review Press.

United Way of America

Approximately fourteen hundred United Way agencies throughout America, made up primarily of volunteers, help meet human and health-care needs through a vast network of local charitable groups and volunteers. Each United Way agency is an independent community resource governed by a local board of volunteers. Through a single community-wide campaign, a United Way agency raises funds to help meet local needs.

However, a United Way agency does much more than raise funds. One of its major services is to promote volunteerism through recruitment and training. When volunteers are uncertain about where they would like to serve, their local United Way agency can give them valuable suggestions. Through United Way, more than three hundred thousand people a year volunteer.

Volunteering Leads to Jobs

Some social service organizations have only a small number of paid staff positions. When a paid position does become available, the applicant who gets the job is frequently a volunteer who has worked for the organization and is thoroughly familiar with its activities. Having experience is often the key to getting a job at a social service organization or government agency, and volunteer work does count as experience. Furthermore, volunteer experience provides networking opportunities, through which a volunteer may hear about job vacancies. The following examples demonstrate that the path to a paid position often begins with a volunteer opportunity.

Big Brothers Big Sisters

Regina Neu is the executive director of the San Francisco and Peninsula agency of Big Brothers Big Sisters. While she has held many responsible positions in the workplace, such as executive director of Young Audiences of the Bay Area and director of community education for an art college, her volunteer experience was a definite plus in obtaining her present position.

Through being a Big Sister to three girls in the Big Brothers Big Sisters Program and serving on the board of a Big Brothers Big Sisters agency, Regina knew the value of this program and how it worked. She has not just volunteered with Big Brothers Big Sisters but has also been a tutor, helped in Girl Scouts programs, and been active in programs in children's hospitals, to name just a few of her many volunteer activities. Regina firmly believes that the skills that you learn as a volunteer can translate into job skills.

American Cancer Society

Claudia Johnson has always had jobs that involved humanitarian activities. She has worked in a hospital as a medical technologist and in Women's Health Resource Centers. About six years ago, Claudia began to work as a volunteer at the Walnut Creek, California, branch of the American Cancer Society, where she became involved in educating the public about cancer. Her primary responsibilities were teaching women about breast cancer and how to do self-examinations and working in antismoking campaigns. Because she had outstanding credentials and the organization knew her and what she could do through her volunteer work, Claudia was hired when a position became available. She especially likes this job because it gives her an opportunity to work directly with people.

Arkansas Division of Volunteerism

Selena Ellis is sold on volunteerism. Today, she is the creator of and program manager for the Arkansas Mentors Program, which recruits volunteers to serve as positive role models and provide one-on-one support to those families who are moving from welfare to independence. Because of welfare reform, organizations across the country are contacting Selena about her program. She also served as a delegate to President Clinton's summit on volunteering. In addition, she is the secretary/treasurer of the National Assembly of State Offices of Volunteerism. It was her experiences in managing volunteer activities for the Junior Auxiliary, Girl Scouts, Red Cross, Cub Scouts, and her church that helped her land a job with the State Office of Volunteerism in Arkansas.

Mennonite Voluntary Service Employee

When David Orr became the personnel director of Mennonite Voluntary Service, he assumed responsibility for recruitment and placement of the one hundred volunteers in the program. While working as a waiter in a Grand Canyon restaurant after college graduation, David's religious convictions motivated him to look for volunteer work. He wanted to put Bible teachings into practice. Through MVS, David started volunteering in youth ministry for two small Mennonite congregations, doing the traditional youth ministry work. He also became involved in helping troubled youths in the community. After volunteering for nearly three years, a job opened up on the national staff of the Mennonite Voluntary Service. David got this job, which ultimately led to his becoming the personnel director. Today, he continues his work as a Good Samaritan as the pastor of a church.

Saint Augustine Home for the Aged Employee

Volunteering two hours a week to visit with an aged blind man was Ann Gisler's introduction to volunteering when she was thirteen years old. For a year, she not only paid Duke Cravens weekly visits at the Saint Augustine's Home for the Aged, but she also shared holidays with him. Their close friendship ended with Duke's death. However, Ann's dedication to helping others was noticed by the Little Sisters of the Poor, who run the home. She was given a paying job at the home, serving food each weekend.

The Age of Volunteering

No one age group has a monopoly on volunteering. Although senior citizens devote the most hours, young people are showing an overwhelming interest in volunteering. It is becoming increasingly popular for high school and college students to devote time to volunteer work. Many high schools are initiating a class in community service that gives students a chance to make some type of change in their communities. At DePauw University, students have the option of spending a month during the interim term (January) doing volunteer service throughout the world.

Throughout the United States, people have found volunteering to be a rewarding experience for both participants and recipients. A vast number of opportunities to serve as a volunteer exist. To find the perfect volunteer spot for yourself, you can become more familiar with the possibilities by reading the following books:

Blaustein, Arthur I. *Make a Difference: Your Guide to Community Service and Volunteering*. Heyday Books, 2002.

Jones, Ellis; Ross Haenfler; and Brett Johnson. *The Better World Handbook: From Good Intentions to Everyday Actions*. New York: New Society Publishers, 2001.

Pybus, Victoria. *The International Directory of Voluntary Work*, 9th ed. Vacation Work Publications, 2005.

CHAPTER SEVEN

Exploring More Careers for Good Samaritans and Humanitarians

"The best way to find yourself is to lose yourself in the service of others."
—Gandhi

Throughout the United States, Good Samaritans and humanitarians are increasingly eager to find careers that center more on making the world better and giving themselves satisfaction than on making a lot of money. Here are a few more careers that would be quite satisfying to people who want to improve the lives of others.

Foundations

Benjamin Franklin was a philanthropist who established a fund to aid worthy young men. Many people with large fortunes, like John D. Rockefeller and Andrew Carnegie, have established foundations to carry out work for the public good. But it isn't just wealthy individuals who establish foundations; families, communities, concerned individuals, and corporations also do so. Foundations vary in size—from the billions of dollars in assets of the

Ford Foundation to the many foundations with assets of less than $100,000. Today, there are more than thirty-eight thousand foundations giving more than $10 billion a year in charitable contributions.

Foundations operate by giving grants to organizations, by operating their own programs, or by a combination of awarding grants and running their own programs. You see foundations in action when you watch public television; many programs are supported by foundation money. Foundations support art museums, civil rights groups, colleges, environmental action groups, food distribution programs, hospitals, housing and health programs, programs for the homeless, research groups, symphony orchestras, and just about every other need that exists. Foundations brought about the development of the Salk polio vaccine, the beginnings of the Head Start program, and the production of "Sesame Street."

Jobs in Foundations

Most of the jobs in foundations are involved with handing out funds. This entails reading and reviewing proposals by fund seekers and doing a lot of routine office work. Unless a foundation operates its own programs, very few jobs involve direct contact with those in need.

Nevertheless, foundation staff members find job satisfaction in working for organizations that assist people and support worthy causes. And top executives do have the opportunity to determine where money will be granted. The smaller the corporation, the greater the likelihood that the staff organization will be informal and staff members will share decisions about where funds will be granted.

To learn which foundations might have career appeal, Good Samaritans and humanitarians should study foundation directories in library reference sections. These directories provide information about each foundation's purpose and activities, background, program areas, finances, and staff size, along with an address for inquiries. Suggested directories include three books published by the Foundation Center in New York: *National Directory of Corporate Giving*, *The National Data Book of Foundations*, and *The Foundation Directory*. To learn more about what working for a foundation is like, read the latest issue of *Foundation News & Commentary* magazine or visit the Council on Foundations website at www.cof.org, which provides information about local and national foundations.

The number of employees at foundations varies greatly, from the Ford Foundation with hundreds of employees to a one-person operation. Seventy-five percent of all foundations are small and unstaffed and are run by volunteers or professionals with jobs in other areas. In recent years, more paid positions have become available at foundations; however, there is considerable competition for these jobs. Most employees at foundations obtain their positions because they have been volunteers with the organization or have networked with people who worked there or knew someone who did.

Working for a Specific Cause

One-on-one involvement with the needy is not the only way Good Samaritans and humanitarians can improve the well-being of people. Working for a social cause or change is also an effective way to do something that benefits society. While the profile of social action groups is lower than it was in the 1960s, many groups are actively working for change—from cleaning up the environment to lobbying for arts education in schools.

Most of these social-cause organizations have a much larger number of volunteers than paid staff. Some of the well-known organizations include the Sierra Club, the Audubon Society, the National Wildlife Federation, Greenpeace, Planned Parenthood, MADD (Mothers Against Drunk Driving), and the American Civil Liberties Union.

Good Samaritans and humanitarians interested in careers in social change should look at *Good Works: A Guide to Careers in Social Change*, published by Barricade Books in New York. *Good Works* is designed to connect idealism with employment. The book lists hundreds of social change organizations in such fields of interest as civil liberties, the emotionally and physically handicapped, health, minorities, senior citizens, urban problems, women, and youth. It also lists other related directories, training schools, and accredited degree programs.

For those interested in a job with an advocacy organization, *Public Interest Group Profiles*, published by the Congressional Quarterly Press and the Foundation for Public Affairs, provides a description of the 250 leading public interest groups. The individual profiles will tell you not only where these groups are located and how to contact them, but also the groups' staff sizes, budgets, purposes, recent publications, members of the board of directors, political orientations, and methods of operation. There are even quoted third-party evaluations of the effectiveness of the groups. You can find *Public Interest Group Profiles* in law school libraries, placement libraries, some public libraries, and a few bookstores.

More Human Services Opportunities

Teachers

Teaching is another job niche that Good Samaritans and humanitarians should explore. While every teaching job obviously involves helping both students and society, some teaching jobs reach special groups of particularly needy students. Included in this category are the physically handicapped, emotionally disturbed, mentally retarded, and socially impaired. In addition to jobs for certified teachers, there are often jobs for aides in special-needs classrooms.

Because of the federal Education Act for All Handicapped Children, teachers are required to develop an individualized learning plan for each child. This requires a close relationship between teachers and individual students, for which many Good Samaritans and humanitarians are well suited. Besides having a bachelor's degree, special certification is frequently required to teach these needy groups of students. Many states require a master's degree in special education.

Job Outlook and Earnings. At present, the outlook is excellent for special education teachers, as the number of students needing these services is increasing. Also, more programs are being created to help students because of growing public interest in students with special needs and legislation emphasizing training and employment for people with disabilities. The salaries of special education teachers generally follow the same scale as for other teachers. The estimated average salary for special education teachers is about $42,000 a year.

Lawyers

The needy are often victims—victims of abuse within their marriages, victims of landlords, victims of merchants, and victims of government service agencies. Legal-aid societies provide the legal help these people need. Clients receive free help if they meet certain financial guidelines, and the society provides the particular services they need. The priority areas for giving help are:

- consumer aid—wage garnishments, bait-and-switch tactics, and collection practices
- family law—divorce, abuse, and custody
- government benefits—getting assistance one is entitled to
- housing—subsidized housing issues, some evictions, and a limited number of foreclosures

Employees of most legal-aid agencies are full-time, paid workers. In addition to lawyers, many legal secretaries, intake workers, paralegals, and client services coordinators work for legal-aid agencies. Most of these jobs involve direct contact with needy clients. For example, client-services coordinators will talk to people when they initially request help, present cases to attorneys, and refer people to other agencies when a legal-aid society is unable to help them.

Many lawyers engaged in private practice do pro bono work, or work for the public good. This involves providing legal services to those who cannot afford them. Often, clients are referred to these lawyers by legal-aid societies. Some of these lawyers work evenings in legal-advice clinics seeing clients; they also go to court with clients if necessary. Yet another category of lawyers who work for the public good are public defenders, court-appointed lawyers who help people accused of crimes who cannot afford private attorneys.

To practice law in any state or other jurisdiction, you will need to be licensed or admitted to its bar. To qualify for the bar examination, an applicant must usually have completed at least three years of college and graduated from a law school approved by the American Bar Association. Competition for admission to many law schools is intense. Paralegals typically have degrees from college paralegal programs or paralegal certificates from formal training programs.

Salaries of experienced lawyers vary greatly. The average salary of beginning lawyers is about $44,000 a year. The beginning salary for paralegals ranges from a low of $24,500 to about $37,000.

Meeting Special Needs

Poverty, hunger, illness, homelessness—Good Samaritans and humanitarians have always responded to these problems. In each generation, however, new needs emerge, such as the need for groups to combat drug and alcohol abuse, and groups to minister to victims of AIDS. Good Samaritans and humanitarians always see new needs and respond to them.

Citizens Energy Corporation

Joseph P. Kennedy II saw that the poor and elderly in Massachusetts needed heating oil to keep their homes comfortable in the winter but that they found it difficult, if not impossible, to pay for this basic need. In 1979, he created Citizens Energy Corporation. This nonprofit oil company eliminated intermediaries and supplied heating oil to the needy at greatly reduced prices through the Massachusetts fuel assistance program. The slogan for the corporation was, "No one should be left out in the cold."

While the first efforts of the corporation were centered on heating oil, in the 1980s Citizens expanded into aiding families with energy emergencies in natural gas and electric power. Because the corporation's mission is to make life's necessities more affordable and available to needy families in the United States and overseas, efforts have been made to make health care more affordable. Recent initiatives have set up a grant program for community-based health programs. Also, the Angola Educational Assistance Fund has been established to rebuild that country's educational structure, and a Women's Opportunity Fund provides loans to help extremely poor women in developing countries establish their own small businesses.

Citizens Energy Corporation founder Joe Kennedy went on to become a congressman from the Eighth Congressional District in Massachusetts. The goal of the corporation remains the same, however: to use entrepreneurial skill to help people in need.

Helping Families Visit Prisons

Cecelia and James Whitfield are individuals who saw a unique need and filled that need. The Whitfields, who were supportive parents, were devastated when their son was imprisoned for robbery. They could have remained heartbroken, but instead they turned their heartbreak into a community service.

Upon visiting their son in prison, the Whitfields quickly learned about the difficulties families and friends of prisoners had making regular visits to the prison. For example, many prisons in their state are quite distant from where the prisoners' families live and are not easily accessible by public transportation. The couple learned of one mother who had not seen her son in five years because friends and family members were always too busy to provide her with the necessary transportation.

With their own money and donations they received, the Whitfields bought a sixty-six-passenger school bus. They began transporting families and friends of prisoners to prisons throughout the state. A monthly schedule was devised, pickup points were established, and a phone number was announced so that people could arrange for transportation. Cecelia's uncle became the bus driver, and either Cecelia or James was aboard on each trip. Their mission was to help loved ones have better relationships with the prisoners. During the trips, the Whitfields encouraged the passengers to share their feelings and support each other. In 1995, the Whitfields switched to a fifteen-passenger van that Cecelia or a volunteer drives to different prisons three times a week, logging twenty-seven thousand miles a year.

Before becoming involved in helping people visit prisoners, neither Cecelia nor James had done any volunteer work except with activities of their children. The good feelings emanating from helping this forgotten segment of the population have prompted the Whitfields to increase their volunteer activities. Today, they are trying to establish a home for women coming out of prison. The Whitfields' goal is to find a way to help these women get off to a good start after leaving prison.

Children's Organ Transplant Association

In 1980, Dave Cain retired at the age of thirty-nine only to find himself years later working eighty-hour weeks in his efforts to raise money for organ transplants. It all began when Dave learned about a two-year-old boy who needed a liver transplant and a family who did not have the money to pay for it. Dave fell in love with the boy and within two months had organized a fund-raising campaign that brought in $100,000.

Unfortunately, the child died, but Dave had a new purpose in life. Since then, his Children's Organ Transplant Association (COTA) has helped several thousand people, mostly children, receive organ transplants. This year COTA is involved in three hundred campaigns across the nation helping people raise money for transplants, which can range in price from $75,000 to $500,000. The organization gives family members and friends of children needing transplants the know-how to conduct fund-raising campaigns in their communities.

Besides raising money for transplants, Dave is working to encourage more people to become organ donors. The need is overwhelming, with fifty-five thousand on the waiting list for organs and many dying because organs are simply not available. His goal is to not have a single person on a donor waiting list before he dies. Dave's volunteer efforts were recognized by President Bush, who gave him the Jefferson Award.

Overview of Job Opportunities

If you were to sit down and try to count the nonprofit organizations in the United States, the task would be nearly impossible—there are over 1.3 million of them. Of course, not all nonprofit organizations minister directly to the needy, but a very high percentage do. Add to this number all the federal, state, and local agencies that are concerned with the welfare of United States citizens, plus the international organizations, and you are looking at an immense number of career and volunteer opportunities for Good Samaritans and other humanitarian types. Americans are caring people who want to help the sick, handicapped, homeless, poor, battered, and needy. Your assistance in this important field would be more than welcomed, and you will gain fulfillment from having a career that truly makes a difference in the lives of others.

InterAction
Member Agencies

nterAction is a coalition of more than 150 nonprofit organizations based in the United States and working to promote human dignity and development in 165 countries around the world. In the United States, we call these groups "private and voluntary organizations," or PVOs. InterAction's diverse membership is active in programs to ease human suffering and to strengthen people's abilities to help themselves. InterAction coordinates and promotes these activities and helps to ensure that goals are met in an ethical and cost-efficient manner. The following list provides you with the addresses of selected member agencies, as well as other PVOs. By visiting the InterAction website at www.interaction.org, you can link directly to the home pages of many of the member agencies.

Academy for Educational Development
1825 Connecticut Avenue NW
Washington, DC 20009
www.aed.org

Accion International
56 Roland Street, Suite 300
Boston, MA 02143
www.accion.org

ACDI/VOCA
50 F Street NW, Suite 1100
Washington, DC 20001
www.acdivoca.org

Action Against Hunger USA
247 West Thirty-Seventh Street, Suite 1207
New York, NY 10018
www.aah-usa.org

ActionAid International USA
1112 Sixteenth Street NW, Suite 540
Washington, DC 20036
www.actionaidusa.org

Adventist Development and Relief Agency (ADRA)
   International
12501 Old Columbia Pike
Silver Spring, MD 20904
www.adra.org

Advocacy Institute
1629 K Street NW, Suite 200
Washington, DC 20006
www.advocacy.org

African Medical and Research Foundation
19 West Forty-Fourth Street, Room 710
New York, NY 10036
www.amref.org

African-American Institute
Graybar Building
420 Lexington Avenue, Suite 1706
New York, NY 10179
www.aaionline.org

Africare
440 R Street NW
Washington, DC 20001
www.africare.org

Aga Khan Foundation
PO Box 2049
1–3 Avenue de la Paix
1211 Geneva 2
Switzerland
www.akdn.org

Aid to Artisans
331 Wethersfield Avenue
Hartford, CT 06114
www.aidtoartisans.org

Alan Guttmacher Institute (AGI)
1301 Connecticut Avenue NW, Suite 700
Washington, DC 20036
www.agi-usa.org

American Jewish Joint Distribution Committee
711 Third Avenue, Tenth Floor
New York, NY 10017
www.jdc.org

American Jewish World Service
45 West Thirty-Sixth Street, Tenth Floor
New York, NY 10018
www.ajws.org

American Near East Refugee Aid (ANERA)
1522 K Street NW, Suite 202
Washington, DC 20005
www.anera.org

American Red Cross
National Headquarters
2025 E Street NW
Washington, DC 20006
www.redcross.org

American Refugee Committee International
430 Oak Grove Street
Minneapolis, MN 55403
www.archq.org

America's Development Foundation (ADF)
101 North Union Street, Suite 200
Alexandria, VA 22314
www.adfusa.org

Amigos de las Américas
5618 Star Lane
Houston, TX 77057
www.amigoslink.org

Ananda Marga Universal Relief Team (AMURT USA)
6517 Cambridge Road
Willowbrook, IL 60527
www.amurt.org

Armenian Assembly of America
1140 Nineteenth Street NW, Suite 600
Washington, DC 20036
www.aaainc.org

Baptist World Alliance
PO Box 6412
Falls Church, VA 22040
www.bwanet.org

Bread for the World
50 F Street NW, Suite 500
Washington, DC 20001
www.bread.org

Brother's Brother Foundation
1200 Galveston Avenue
Pittsburgh, PA 15233
www.brothersbrother.org

CARE
151 Ellis Street NE
Atlanta, GA 30303
www.careusa.org

Catholic Medical Mission Board
10 West Seventeenth Street
New York, NY 10011
www.cmmb.org

Catholic Relief Services
209 West Fayette Street
Baltimore, MD 21201
www.catholicrelief.org

Center for International Health and Cooperation (CIHC)
Fordham University
113 West Sixtieth Street, LL224E
New York, NY 10021
www.cihc.org

Center of Concern
1225 Otis Street NE
Washington, DC 20017
www.coc.org

Centre for Development and Population Activities (CEDPA)
1133 Twenty-First Street NW, Suite 800
Washington, DC 20036
www.cedpa.org

Child Health Foundation
10630 Little Patuxent Parkway, Suite 126
Columbia, MD 21044
www.childhealthfoundation.org

Childreach/Plan International
155 Plan Way
Warwick, RI 02886
www.childreach.org

Christian Children's Fund (CCF)
2821 Emerywood Parkway
Richmond, VA 23294
www.christianchildrensfund.org

Christian Reformed World Relief Committee (CRWRC)
2850 Kalamazoo Avenue SE
Grand Rapids, MI 49560
www.crwrc.org

Church World Service (CWS)
475 Riverside Drive
New York, NY 10115
www.churchworldservice.org

Citizens Network for Foreign Affairs
1828 L Street NW, Suite 710
Washington, DC 20036
www.cnfa.org

Counterpart International
1200 Eighteenth Street NW, Suite 1100
Washington, DC 20036
www.counterpart.org

Direct Relief International
27 South La Patera Lane
Santa Barbara, CA 93117
www.directrelief.org

Doctors of the World
375 West Broadway, Fourth Floor
New York, NY 10012
www.doctorsoftheworld.org

Doctors Without Borders
333 Seventh Avenue, Second Floor
New York, NY 10001
www.doctorswithoutborders.org

Empowering Community Development International
2300 Vernon Circle
Minnetonka, MN 55305
www.ecdinternational.org

Enersol Associates, Inc.
55 Middlesex Street, Suite 221
North Chelmsford, MA 01863
www.enersol.org

Enterprise Development International
10395-B Democracy Lane
Fairfax, VA 22030
www.endpoverty.org

EnterpriseWorks/VITA (Volunteers in Technical Assistance)
1825 Connecticut Avenue NW, Suite 630
Washington, DC 20009
www.enterpriseworks.org

Episcopal Migration Ministries
815 Second Avenue
New York, NY 10017
www.episcopalchurch.org

Food for the Hungry, Inc.
1124 East Washington Street
Phoenix, AZ 85034
www.fh.org

FINCA International (Foundation for International
    Community Assistance)
1101 Fourteenth Street NW, Suite 1100
Washington, DC 20005
www.villagebanking.org

Freedom from Hunger (FFH)
1644 DaVinci Court
Davis, CA 95616
www.freefromhunger.org

Goodwill Industries International
15810 Indianola Drive
Rockville, MD 20855
www.goodwill.org

Grassroots International
179 Boylston Street, Fourth Floor
Boston, MA 02130
www.grassrootsonline.org

Health Volunteers Overseas (HVO)
1900 L Street NW, Suite 310
Washington, DC 20036
www.hvousa.org

Heifer Project International
PO Box 8058
Little Rock, AR 72203
www.heifer.org

Helen Keller International (HKI)
352 Park Avenue South, Twelfth Floor
New York, NY 10010
www.hki.org

Hebrew Immigrant Aid Society (HIAS)
333 Seventh Avenue, Sixteenth Floor
New York, NY 10001
www.hias.org

Holt International Children's Services
1195 City View
Eugene, OR 97402
www.holtintl.org

The Hunger Project
15 East Twenty-Sixth Street
New York, NY 10010
www.thp.org

Institute of Cultural Affairs (ICA)
4750 North Sheridan Road
Chicago, IL 60640
www.ica-usa.org

Interchurch Medical Assistance
PO Box 429
New Windsor, MD 21776
www.interchurch.org

International Aid, Inc.
17011 West Hickory
Spring Lake, MI 49456
http://internationalaid.gospelcom.net

International Catholic Migration Commission (ICMC)
3211 Fourth Street NE
Washington, DC 20017
www.icmc.net

International Center for Research on Women
1717 Massachusetts Avenue NW, Suite 302
Washington, DC 20036
www.icrw.org

International City/County Management Association
777 North Capitol Street NE, Suite 500
Washington, DC 20002
www.icma.org

International Executive Service Corps
901 Fifteenth Street NW, Suite 1010
Washington, DC 20005
www.iesc.org

International Eye Foundation (IEF)
10801 Connecticut Aveunue
Kennington, MD 20895
www.iefusa.org

International Institute of Rural Reconstruction (IIRR)
333 East Thirty-Eighth Street, Sixth Floor
New York, NY 10116
www.iirr.org

International Medical Corps (IMC)
1919 Santa Monica Blvd, Suite 300
Santa Monica, CA 90404
www.imcworldwide.org

INMED Partnerships for Children
45449 Severn Way, Suite 161
Sterling, VA 22170
www.inmed.org

International Orthodox Christian Charities (IOCC)
110 West Road, Suite 360
Baltimore, MD 21204
www.iocc.org

International Reading Association (IRA)
800 Barksdale Road
Newark, DE 19714
www.reading.org

International Rescue Committee (IRC)
122 East Forty-Second Street
New York, NY 10168
www.theirc.org

International Voluntary Service
5505 Walnut Level Road
Crozet, VA 22932
www.sci-ivs.org

International Women's Health Coalition
333 Seventh Avenue, Sixth Floor
New York, NY 10001
www.iwhc.org

Jesuit Refugee Service/U.S.A. (JRS/USA)
1616 P Street NW, Suite 300
Washington, DC 20036
www.jesref.org

Katalysis North/South Development Partnership
1331 North Commerce Street
Stockton, CA 95202
www.katalysis.org

LDS Philanthropies
15 East South Temple Street, Second Floor East
Salt Lake City, UT 84150
www.lds.org

Lutheran Immigration and Refugee Service (LIRS)
700 Light Street
Baltimore, MD 21230
www.lirs.org

Lutheran World Relief (LWR)
700 Light Street
Baltimore, MD 21230
www.lwr.org

Map International
2200 Glynco Parkway, Box 50
Brunswick, GA 31521
www.map.org

March of Dimes Birth Defects Foundation
1275 Mamaroneck Avenue
White Plains, NY 10605
www.marchofdimes.com

Medical Care Development (MCD)
11 Parkwood Drive
Augusta, ME 04330
www.mcd.org

Mercy Corps International (MCI)
3015 Southwest First Avenue
Portland, OR 97201
www.mercycorps.org

National Council of Negro Women
633 Pennsylvania Avenue NW
Washington, DC 20004
www.ncnw.org

National Peace Corps Association
1900 L Street NW, Suite 205
Washington, DC 20036
www.rpcv.org

National Wildlife Federation (NWF)
11100 Wildlife Center Drive
Reston, VA 20190
www.nwf.org

Near East Foundation
90 Broad Street, Fifteenth Floor
New York, NY 10004
www.neareast.org

OIC International (Opportunities Industrialization Centers)
240 West Tulpehocken Street
Philadelphia, PA 19144
www.oicinternational.org

Operation U.S.A.
8320 Melrose Avenue, Suite 200
Los Angeles, CA 90069
www.opusa.org

Opportunity International
2122 York Road
Oakbrook, IL 60523
www.opportunity.org

Outreach International
PO Box 210
Independence, MO 64051
www.outreach-international.org

Oxfam America
26 West Street
Boston, MA 02111
www.oxfamamerica.org

Pact
1220 Eighteenth Street NW, Suite 350
Washington, DC 20036
www.pactworld.org

Partners of the Americas
1424 K Street NW, Suite 700
Washington, DC 20005
www.partners.net

Pathfinder International
9 Galen Street, Suite 217
Watertown, MA 02172
www.pathfind.org

Pax World Service
Department Pax
PO Box 2669
Portland, OR 97205
www.paxworld.org

The Pearl S. Buck Foundation
520 Dublin Road
Perkasie, PA 18944
www.pearl-s-buck.org

Physicians for Human Rights
Two Arrow Street, Suite 301
Cambridge, MA 02138
www.phrusa.org

Physicians for Peace
229 West Bute Street, Suite 200
Norfolk, VA 23510
www.physiciansforpeace.org

Planned Parenthood of New York City
Margaret Sanger Square
26 Bleecker Street
New York, NY 10012
www.ppnyc.org

Points of Light Foundation
1400 I Street NW, Suite 800
Washington, DC 20005
www.pointsoflight.org

Population Action International
1300 Nineteenth Street NW, Second Floor
Washington, DC 20036
www.populationaction.org

Presbyterian Disaster Assistance and Hunger Program
100 Witherspoon Street
Louisville, KY 40202
www.pcusa.org/hunger

Proliteracy Worldwide
1320 Jamesville Avenue
Syracuse, NY 13210
www.proliteracy.org

Refugees International
1705 N Street NW
Washington, DC 20036
www.refugeesinternational.org

Relief International
1575 Westwood Boulevard, Suite 201
Los Angeles, CA 90024
www.ri.org

Results, Inc.
440 First Street NW, Suite 450
Washington, DC 20001
www.results.org

Salvation Army World Service Office (SAWSO)
615 Slaters Lane
Alexandria, VA 22313
www.salvationarmyusa.org

Save the Children
54 Wilton Road
Westport, CT 06880
www.savethechildren.org

Service and Development Agency (SADA) of the African
   Methodist Episcopal Church
1134 Eleventh Street NW, Suite 214
Washington, DC 20001
www.amecnet.org

Share Foundation
598 Bosworth Street, Number 1
San Francisco, CA 94131
www.share-elsalvador.org

Sierra Club
85 Second Street, Second Floor
San Francisco, CA 94105
www.sierraclub.org

Society of St. Andrew
3383 Sweet Hollow Road
Big Island, VA 24526
www.endhunger.org

Solar Cookers International
1919 Twenty-First Street, Suite 101
Sacramento, CA 95814
www.solarcookers.org

Southeast Asia Resource Action Center (SEARAC)
1628 Sixteenth Street NW, Third Floor
Washington, DC 20009
www.searac.org

Synergos Institute
9 East Sixty-Ninth Street
New York, NY 10021
www.synergos.org

Technoserve
49 Day Street
Norwalk, CT 06854
www.technoserve.org

Tolstoy Foundation
PO Box 578
Valley Cottage, NY 10989
www.tolstoyfoundation.org

Trickle Up Program
104 West Twenty-Seventh Street, Twelfth Floor
New York, NY 10001
www.trickleup.org

Unitarian Universalist Service Committee (UUSC)
130 Prospect Street
Cambridge, MA 02139
www.uusc.org

United Jewish Communities
PO Box 30
Old Chelsea Station
New York, NY 10013
www.ujc.org

United Way International
701 North Fairfax Street
Alexandria, VA 22314
www.uwint.org

U.S. Association for the United Nations High Commissioner
   for Refugees (USA for UNHCR)
1775 K Street NW, Suite 290
Washington, DC 20006
www.usaforunhcr.org

U.S. Committee for Refugees and Immigrants
1717 Massachusetts Avenue NW, Second Floor
Washington, DC 20036
www.refugees.org

U.S. Conference of Catholic Bishops
3211 Fourth Street NE
Washington, DC 20017
www.usccb.org

U.S. Fund for UNICEF
333 East Thirty-Eighth Street
New York, NY 10016
www.unicefusa.org

Winrock International
2101 Riverfront Drive
Little Rock, AR 72202
www.winrock.org

Women's American ORT Federation (Organization for
Educational Resources and Technological Training)
250 Park Avenue South
New York, NY 10003
www.waort.org

World Concern
19303 Fremont Avenue North
Seattle, WA 98133
www.worldconcern.org

World Education Services
Bowling Green Station
PO Box 5087
New York, NY 10274
www.wes.org

World Learning
Kipling Road
PO Box 676
Brattleboro, VT 05301
www.worldlearning.org

World Neighbors
4127 NW 122nd Street
Oklahoma City, OK 73120
www.wn.org

World Relief
7 East Baltimore Street
Baltimore, MD 21200
www.wr.org

World Resources Institute (WRI)
10 G Street NE, Suite 800
Washington, DC 20002
www.wri.org

World Vision
PO Box 9716
Federal Way, WA 98063
www.worldvision.org

World Wildlife Fund (WWF)
1250 Twenty-Fourth Street NW
Washington, DC 20037
www.worldwildlife.org

Young Men's Christian Association (YMCA)
101 North Wacker Drive
Chicago, IL 60606
www.ymca.net

Young Women's Christian Association (YWCA)
Empire State Building, Suite 301
New York, NY 10118
www.ywca.org

Zero Population Growth (ZPG)
1400 Sixteenth Street NW, Suite 320
Washington, DC 20036
www.populationconnection.org

Missionary Organizations

The following organizations will provide you with information about serving overseas as a missionary:

Episcopal Church's World Mission
Episcopal Church Center
815 Second Avenue
New York, NY 10017
www.episcopalchurch.org

Evangelical Lutheran Church in America
8765 West Higgins Road
Chicago, IL 60631
www.elca.org

General Board of Global Ministries
The United Methodist Church
475 Riverside Drive
New York, NY 10115
www.gbgm-umc.org

Global Ministries
PO Box 1986
Indianapolis, IN 46216
www.globalministries.org

International Ministries
PO Box 851
Valley Forge, PA 19482
www.internationalministries.org

International Mission Board
Southern Baptist Convention
3806 Monument Avenue
PO Box 6767
Richmond, VA 23230
www.imb.org

Presbyterian Church in America
1700 North Brown Road
Lawrenceville, GA 30043
www.pcanet.org

Reformed Church in America
4500 Sixtieth Street SE
Grand Rapids, MI 49512
www.rca.org

U.S. Conference of Catholic Bishops
3211 Fourth Street NE
Washington, DC 20017
www.usccb.org

Worldwide Ministries Division of the Presbyterian Church
100 Witherspoon Street
Louisville, KY 40202
www.pcusa.org/wmd

You can obtain additional addresses from the directory of churches in the *Yearbook of American and Canadian Churches* (Abingdon Press).

State Offices of Volunteerism

The following state offices of volunteerism will provide you with helpful information about volunteering opportunities in your home state. States not listed do not have an office of volunteerism.

ALABAMA

Governor's Office of Faith-Based and Community Initiatives
100 North Union Street, Suite 134
Montgomery, AL 36104
www.goncs.state.al.us

ALASKA

Alaska State Community Service Commission
550 West Seventh Street
Anchorage, AK 99501
www.dced.state.ak.us/ascsc

ARIZONA

Governor's Commission on Service and Volunteerism
1700 West Washington Street, Suite 101
Phoenix, AZ 85007
www.volunteerarizona.org

ARKANSAS
Arkansas Department of Health and Human Services
Division of Volunteerism
Donaghey Plaza, Seventh and Main Streets
Little Rock, AR 72203
www.state.ar.us/dhs/adov

CALIFORNIA
Volunteer Centers of California
1110 K Street, Suite 210
Sacramento, CA 95814
www.volunteercentersca.org

COLORADO
Governor's Commission on Community Service
1059 Alton Way
Building 758, Suite 253
Denver, CO 80203
www.colorado.gov/gccs

CONNECTICUT
Connecticut Commission on National and Community
    Service (CCNCS)
Connecticut Department of Higher Education
61 Woodland Street
Hartford, CT 06105
www.ct.gov

DELAWARE
State Office of Volunteerism
Division of State Service Centers
1901 North Dupont Highway
Charles Debnam Building
New Castle, DE 19720
www.dhss.delaware.gov/dhss/volopps.html

DISTRICT OF COLUMBIA
Serve DC
441 Fourth Street NW, Suite 1040S
Washington, DC 20001
www.cncs.dc.gov

FLORIDA
Volunteer Florida
Governor's Commission on Volunteerism and Community
  Service
Elliot Building
401 South Monroe Street
Tallahassee, FL 32301
www.volunteerflorida.org

GEORGIA
Georgia Commission for Service and Volunteerism
Georgia DCA
60 Executive Park South NE
Atlanta, GA 30329
www.dca.state.ga.us/communities/Volunteerism

HAWAII
Hawaii State Volunteer Services
Liliuokalani Center for Student Services
2600 Campus Road, Room 414
Honolulu, HI 96822
www.hawaii.gov

Volunteer Resource Center of Hawaii at University of Hawaii
Winward Community College
Hale Alakai Room 106
45–720 Keaahala Road
Kaneohe, HI 96744
www.vrchawaii.org

IDAHO
Serve Idaho
Governor's Commission on Service and Volunteerism
1299 North Orchard Street, Suite 110
Boise, ID 83706
www.serveidaho.com

ILLINOIS
Illinois Commission on Volunteerism and Community Service
535 West Jefferson, Third Floor
Springfield, IL 62702
www.illinois.gov/volunteer

INDIANA
Office of Faith-Based and Community Initiatives
Indiana Government Center South, Room E012
302 West Washington Street
Indianapolis, IN 46204
www.in.gov/iccsv

IOWA
Iowa Commission on Volunteer Services
200 East Grand Avenue
Des Moines, IA 50309
www.volunteeriowa.org

KANSAS
Kanserve
Kansas Volunteer Commission
120 SE Tenth Avenue
Topeka, KS 66612
www.kanserve.org

KENTUCKY

Kentucky Commission on Community Volunteerism and
  Service
275 East Main Street
Frankfort, KY 40621
www.chfs.ky.gov/dhss/kccvs

LOUISIANA

Louisiana Serve Commission
263 Third Street, Suite 610-B
Baton Rouge, LA 70801
www.crt.state.la.us/laserve

MAINE

Maine Commission for Community Service
State Planning Office
187 State Street, 38 State House Station
Augusta, ME 04333
www.maineservicecommission.gov

MARYLAND

Governor's Office on Service and Volunteerism
State Office Center
300 West Preston Street, Suite 608
Baltimore, MD 21201
www.gosv.state.md.us

MASSACHUSETTS

Massachusetts Service Alliance
100 North Washington Street, Third Floor
Boston, MA 02114
www.msalliance.org

MICHIGAN
Michigan Community Service Commission
1048 Pierpont, Suite 4
Lansing, MI 48911
www.michigan.gov/mcsc

MINNESOTA
Serve Minnesota
431 South Seventh Street, Suite 2540
Minneapolis, MN 55415
www.serveminnesota.org

MISSISSIPPI
Mississippi Commission for Volunteer Service
3825 Ridgewood Road, Suite 601
Jackson, MS 39211
www.mcvs.org

MISSOURI
Missouri Community Service Commission
PO Box 118
770 Truman State Office Building
Jefferson City, MO 65102
www.movolunteers.org

MONTANA
Office of Community Service
PO Box 200801
Helena, MT 59620
www.discoveringmontana.com/mcsn

NEBRASKA
Nebraska Volunteer Service Commission
State Capitol, Sixth Floor
PO Box 98927
Lincoln, NE 68509
www.nol.org/home/NVSC

NEVADA
Nevada Commission for National and Community Service
137 Keddie Street
Fallon, NV 89406
www.ncncs.com

NEW HAMPSHIRE
Volunteer NH!
117 Pleasant Street, Fourth Floor
Dolloff Building
Concord, NH 03301
www.volunteernh.org

NEW JERSEY
New Jersey Commission on National and Community Service
Department of Education
PO Box 500
Trenton, NJ 08625
www.state.nj.us

NEW MEXICO
New Mexico Commission for Community Volunteerism
3401 Pan American Freeway NE
Albuquerque, NM 87107
www.newmexserve.org

NEW YORK
New York State Commission on National and Community
  Service
Capital View Office Park
52 Washington Street
Rensselaer, NY 12144
www.nyscncs.org

NORTH CAROLINA
North Carolina Commission on Volunteerism and
  Community Service
Office of the Governor
20312 Mail Service Center
116 West Jones Street
Raleigh, NC 27699
www.volunteernc.org

NORTH DAKOTA
North Dakota Governor's Office
Department 101
600 East Boulevard Avenue
Bismarck, ND 58505
www.governor.state.nd.us

OHIO
Ohio Community Service Council
51 North High Street, Suite 800
Columbus, Ohio 43215
www.serveohio.org

OKLAHOMA
Oklahoma Community Service Commission
1401 North Lincoln Boulevard
Oklahoma City, OK 73104
www.okamericorps.com

OREGON
Oregon Volunteers
1600 SW Fourth Avenue, Suite 850
Portland, OR 97201
www.oregonvolunteers.org

PENNSYLVANIA
PennSERVE: Governor's Office of Citizen Service
1306 Labor and Industry Building, Room 1306
Seventh and Forester Street
Harrisburg, PA 17120
www.pennserve.state.pa.us

PUERTO RICO
Puerto Rico State Commission on Community Service
Department of Education, Tenth Floor
PO Box 190759
San Juan, PR 00919
www.gobierno.pr

RHODE ISLAND
Rhode Island Service Alliance
PO Box 72822
Providence, RI 02905
www.riservicealliance.org

SOUTH CAROLINA
South Carolina Commission on National and Community
    Service
3710 Landmark Drive, Suite 200
Columbia, SC 29204
www.servicesc.org

SOUTH DAKOTA

Governor's Office for Volunteerism
500 East Capitol Avenue
Pierre, SD 57501
www.state.sd.us/governor

TEXAS

Texas Commission on Volunteerism and Community Service
1700 North Congress Avenue, Suite 310
PO Box 13385
Austin, TX 78701
www.twc.state.tx.us

UTAH

Utah Commission on Volunteers
324 South State Street
Salt Lake City, UT 84111
www.volunteers.utah.org

VERMONT

Vermont Commission on National and Community Service
109 State Street
Montpelier, VT 05609
www.state.vt.us/cncs

VIRGINIA

Virginia Commission for National and Community Service
7 North Eighth Street
Richmond, VA 23219
www.vaservice.org

WASHINGTON
Washington Commission for National and Community
  Service
PO Box 43113
Olympia, WA 98504
www.ofm.wa.gov/servwa

WISCONSIN
Wisconsin National and Community Service Board
PO Box 8916
Madison, WI 53708
www.servewisconsin.org

WYOMING
Wyoming Commission on National and Community Service
122 West Twenty-Fifth Street, Room 1609
Herschler Building, First Floor West
Cheyenne, WY 82002
http://wyoming.gov

About the Authors

Marjorie Eberts and Margaret Gisler have been writing together professionally for thirty-one years. They are prolific freelance authors with more than ninety books in print. Besides writing career books, the two authors have written textbooks, beginning readers, and study skills books for school children. They also write a syndicated education column, "Dear Teacher," which appears in newspapers throughout the country.

Writing this book was a special pleasure for the authors, as it gave them the opportunity to meet numerous Good Samaritans and humanitarians who are not only improving the welfare of others but also receiving immense satisfaction from their careers.

Marjorie Eberts is a graduate of Stanford University, and Margaret Gisler is a graduate of Ball State and Butler Universities. Both received their specialist degrees in education from Butler University.

DATE DUE

MAY 12 2009		
4/7/2011		
APR 19 2012		

Ca
HV
10
.E   ns
20   es